# SPICED DELICACIES

## FAMILY RECIPES FROM

## GOA (INDIA)

FRANCIS X. COLAÇO

Dishes prepared in the homes of
Teresa B. da Costa (Goa), Margarida Colaço (Mumbai)
and Marie-Henriette de Pelet-Colaço (Washington, D.C.)

Photographs of dishes in India and some Goan vistas by Martin Colaço.
Photographs of other Goan vistas by Antoine Colaço.
Photographs of dishes in her home by Marie-Henriette de Pelet-Colaço.

Edited by Isabel de Figueiredo, Margarida Colaço and Fatima Colaço.

Manuscript prepared by Marie-Henriette de Pelet-Colaço.

Designed by Julie Dailly

This edition published in 2002.
Printed and bound in Gaithersburg, Maryland, USA
ISBN 0-9726570-0-2

© 2002 by Francis X. Colaço
All rights reserved.
e-mail address : amc.inc@verizon.net

# TABLE OF CONTENTS

**Preface**

I. **Introduction**

　The Land

　Its People and Their Way of Life

　Meals

　Historical Perspective

　A View of the Influences on Goan Cuisine

II. **Spices in Goan Cooking**

III. **Useful tips**

IV. **Goan Recipes**

　A. Soups and Appetizers

　B. Fish and Seafood

　C. Meats and Poultry

　D. Vegetables and Eggs

　E. Rice and Breads

　F. Chutney and Pickles

　G. Desserts, Sweets, and Cookies

　H. Goan Drinks

**Menus**

**Index of Recipes**

**Glossary**

# Weights and Measures
## Conversion Tables

All weights and measures used throughout this book are the ones used in the U.S.A. The table below gives approximate U.K. and metric equivalencies.

### WEIGHTS

| | |
|---|---|
| ½ oz | 15 grams |
| 1 oz | 25 |
| 1½ oz | 40 |
| 2 | 50 |
| 2½ | 65 |
| 3 | 75 |
| 4 | 100 grams |
| 5 | 150 |
| 6 | 175 |
| 8 | 225 |
| 10 | 275 |
| 1 lb | 450 |
| 1 ½ | 750 |
| 3 | 1.5 kg |

### MEASUREMENTS

| | |
|---|---|
| ⅛ inch | 3mm |
| ¼ inch | 0.5 cm |
| ½ inch | 1 cm |
| ¾ inch | 2 |
| 1 inch | 2.5 |
| 1 ½ | 4 |
| 2 | 5 |
| 3 | 7.5 |
| 4 | 10 |
| 5 | 13 |
| 6 | 15 |
| 8 | 20 |
| 10 | 25.5 |
| 12 | 30 |

### LIQUID VOLUMES

| American Cups | British Fl oz | Metric Ml |
|---|---|---|
| ¼ cup | 2 fl oz | 59 ml |
| ⅓ | 3 | 79 ml |
| ½ | 4 | 119 |
| ⅔ | 5 | 157 |
| ¾ | 6 | 178 |
| 1 | 8 | 237 |
| 4 | 1½ pt | 1 liter |

### OVEN TEMPERATURES

| | F | C |
|---|---|---|
| Gas 1 | 275° F | 140° C |
| 2 | 300 | 150 |
| 3 | 325 | 160 |
| 4 | 350 | 180 |
| 5 | 375 | 190 |
| 6 | 400 | 200 |
| 7 | 425 | 220 |
| 8 | 450 | 230 |
| 9 | 475 | 240 |

The British standard tablespoon holds 17.7 milliliters, while the American standard measuring spoon holds 14.2 milliliters. The American and Canadian pint is 16 fluid ounces, as opposed to the British Imperial pint, which is 20 fluid ounces. The American ½ pint measuring cup is therefore equivalent to two-fifths of a British pint. 4 US cups (2 pints or 1 quart) equals 1 ½ British pints.

# PREFACE

Food and music are central to the Goan self-image and are part of the Goan soul. In a Goan household, mouth-watering aromas permeate the house. The smells are an exotic combination of spiced delicacies: saffron, garlic, chilies, tamarind, onions, coriander, cumin, and meat or fish or prawns or crustaceans or vegetables, cooked and tempered and sweetened with coconut. These aromas mix with the smell of cooking rice and draw one to the dining table.

The longing for these spiced delicacies drives the individual Goan expatriate living in a Western Hemisphere country either to take up cooking, or to find someone who can do credit to "our" cuisine so as to establish a long-lasting relationship. Good cooking is definitely the way to a Goan's heart.

Goan cooking is not available in Indian restaurants. There are dishes on menus that are purportedly Goan (for example, Goan fish curry or Goan prawn curry or Goan *vindalho*), capitalizing on the mystique created by the Western tourists' rediscovery of Goa as a prime tourism spot. These dishes are a pale shadow of the real thing. Traditional Goan cooking is found today largely in Goan households. To sample this cuisine, the non-Goan has to cultivate the friendship of a Goan with a reputation for cooking skills. Or, take up cooking himself. This book is constructed to enable the non-Goan to prepare, in a user-friendly manner, this exquisite cuisine.

Cooking recipes in Goa are generally transmitted orally within families. There is no one universally accepted recipe even for the most special Goan dishes. The debate rages furiously about whose recipe is better. It pits one mother's recipes against those of another, and one *mesta's* (or cook's) recipes against those of another's. Distances of time and space accentuate memories of tastes and aromas. There are quasi-irreconcilable debates about personal taste preferences. It is always amusing when two members of the same family debate the merits of a dish with remembered tastes of one's youth or the influence of a taste acquired as a result of a new partner. As Craig Claiborne has put it: "nothing can equal the universal appeal of the food of one's childhood and early youth."

Goans are similar to southern Europeans - the French, the Greeks, the Italians, the Spaniards, and the Portuguese - in one important aspect. Food preparation is a ritual. Food is not only to be consumed, but also to be talked about. Meals are not only an occasion for gastronomy, but also for social and convivial exchanges. The preparation and enjoyment of food is an essential element of culture.

Goan cooking has evolved over the centuries. It has not been the reflection of the genius of individual renowned chefs famous for their starred restaurants or their cookbooks. There is no Goan equivalent of Paul Bocuse, Jacques Pepin, Julia Child, or Alice Waters. But the same kind of talent and creativity, fueled by the love of good food, has influenced the experimentation and combination of ingredients that has evolved over centuries into a very unique form of cuisine. We have imported spices and recipes, modified them with gusto, and enjoyed them with delight. Recipes have been handed down through oral tradition and practice over generations. Cooking took place in private homes. Cooks became renowned, within an extended family and group of friends, for their culinary genius. Recipes were exchanged, sometimes reluctantly, outside the family circle. Restaurants were almost non-existent during the Goan colonial period. Entertaining took place within individual homes. This was not like modern stylized fusion of East-West cuisine. This was high quality cooking of the people, by the people, for the people.

*Alda Ribeiro Colaço*

One of those, whose cooking and dining table became renowned, both in Goa and in Bombay, was Alda Ribeiro Colaço – our late mother and mother-in-law. She was a superlative cook, and an absolutely lovely, cultured and elegant lady. She raised ten children and cultivated in them a taste for elegance and fine things, especially fine Goan food. This book contains her recipes. They were compiled by her family from recipes that, over the years, she sent to her sons and daughters in handwritten letters, and from her handwritten recipes in notebooks. It is for this reason that this book has been a family effort with central contributions by Isabel P. de Figueiredo, Carmen Miranda Colaço, Margarida Colaço, and Teresa B. da Costa. Alda Ribeiro Colaço was a caring and sharing person. We, her family, now take this opportunity to share her love of Goan cuisine and her recipes with a larger audience.

Today, forty years after the end of colonial rule, Goan cuisine exists and flourishes. It has of necessity had to change, as it also did in the past. It now meets the taste requirements of returning expatriates, and of a booming Goan tourist trade from all parts of India and the world. Traditional Goan Christian cuisine is practiced and preserved in the homes of a generation that came to maturity in the post-colonial period. They still remember vividly and with nostalgia their parents' and grandparents' lifestyles. The far-flung Goan Diaspora (there are far more Goan Christians living outside, than inside, Goa and India) clings to the memories of Goan food and music. We indulge in them on feast days in traditional Goan meals and festivals that are held in Dubai or Lisbon or Toronto or Los Angeles or San Francisco or New York or Houston or Washington DC, or wherever there is more than one Goan family. On each occasion, not only is the food and camaraderie enjoyed, but the ageless debate continues about the authentic way of preparing a particular dish. We hope that this book will contribute to that delightful debate. We also hope that it is presented in a form designed to tempt Western lovers of good food to a form of cuisine to which they have not been previously exposed. We have enjoyed this cuisine and are proud of it. We hope that you will be able to share and enjoy it.

# I. INTRODUCTION

In 1961, after four centuries of colonial domination by Portugal, Goa was re-integrated with India, of which it was a physical part. Goan Christians, whose cuisine is described in this book, experienced a major cultural shock. Our language (*konkani*) had Indian roots, but it had absorbed and made our own patois of a number of Portuguese words and expressions. Our music (the *mando*) based on local traditions, also used Portuguese instruments and rhythms and blended and modified these to make them our own. Our physical isolation from India for a number of years, brought on by political forces, had led us to absorb a fair number of Western modes of dress and behavior albeit with our own distinctive flair. Goa had been known for centuries as the *Rome of the Orient* because of its historic churches. It became over time a unique blend of East and West, reflected in the architecture of houses, the richness of its cultural traditions, its music, and above all else the Goan Christian food. Goa has been referred to by visitors as the *Lisbon of India*, *Queen of the Malabar Coast*, and *Goa Dourada* or *Golden Goa*.

## The Land

The travelogues of Europeans who visited Goa in the 16$^{th}$ through 18$^{th}$ centuries, marveled at the port of Goa which they considered one of the finest in Asia. Jean-Baptiste Tavernier noted that Goa is "abound in corn, rice, mangoes, pineapples, bananas, coconuts." Thevenot describes it as "being plentiful in corn, beasts and fruit and hath a great deal of good water." Waves of visitors over the years, continued to be enchanted by the natural beauty of Goa. This has made it a mecca for tourists, with direct air flights from Europe and from different parts of India. Goa is accessible by road and rail; and during the non-monsoon season, by sea.

Goa is located in the middle of the west coast of India, in the tropics, north of the equator. The land area measures about 3700 square kilometers (about the size of the American state of Rhode Island). It is about 60 kilometers wide and about 105 kilometers in length. It lies between a mountain range (the Western Ghats) on the east and the Arabian Sea on the west. As P. P. Srivastava has described it: "…Goa is one cavalcade of natural beauty descending from the Western Ghats to the Arabian Sea. A drive in any direction brings tantalizing glimpses of pools reflecting the sun, trees stretched and etched against the skyline, palatial mansions encircled with greenery, golden beaches, emerald forests, bushes, climbers, creepers. One instinctively feels in tune with nature."

These rhapsodic descriptions of Goa, by visitors over the years, are no exaggeration. Imagine a well-sheltered harbor of Marmagoa, which is the best on the west coast of India. Long and broad beaches covered with fine white sand, dunes and coconut palms through which the wind whispers. Large ocean- and rain-fed rivers (the Mandovi and Zuari) and three other rivers (Terekhol, Chapora, and Betul) which crisscross the land so that one is never very far from the sea and internal waterways. A hilly land sloping to the west and the sea, with spectacular waterfalls. A basically agrarian economy, with a regular supply of sea and river fish and crustaceans. Red soil and green rice paddy fields washed and watered by the torrential southwestern monsoons between late May and August, with annual rain totals of between 90 and 120 inches. Coconut palms growing at the edges of paddy fields, with their luxuriant fronds and succulent green-husked coconuts dangling precariously from their stems. A hot, humid tropical climate with average annual temperatures in the eighties Fahrenheit which contributes to the lushness of the vegetation and the discomfort of humans. Mango trees laden, in March through May, with their ripe, golden, fruit. Cashew trees clinging to the sides of hills with their orange and yellow fruit, the nuts suspended at the bottom. Papaya trees with their golden yellow ripe fruit ready for slicing and eating either at breakfast or as dessert. Jackfruits suspended ponderously from strong sap-laden branches.

This is Goa. A land of scenic beauty. Hills covered with lush vegetation. Beautiful unspoiled beaches skirting a rolling sea. Rivers lined with vegetation and coconut palms. Fishing boats, sail boats, rowboats, barges and ferries navigating the flowing rivers and the sea. Green rice paddy fields contrasting with the rich red color of the lateritic soils. There is an embarrassment of natural riches in a small land area. Goa has become a mecca for the international tourist in the winter months of November through February.

## Its People and Their Way of Life

The population of Goa was 445,000 in 1880 and 590,000 in 1960, just before the end of colonialism. Emigration was a constant feature of Goan life, particularly for Christian Goans, provoked by the search for better educational opportunities and means of livelihood. There was a larger number of Goans in other parts of India and the world, than in Goa. Over 70% of the population was rural, and only 30% urban. In 1960, Christians were about 40% of the total population, and Hindus were 60%. Hindus were the predominant economic group in the urban and mining sectors of the Goan economy. The lower proportion of Christians in the population resident in Goa was heavily influenced by the fact that Christians emigrated from Goa in much higher numbers than did Hindus.

The home was the center of life. Doors were open all through the day, since communities were stable and people knew each other. Crime was at a minimum. One announced one's arrival, not by ringing a doorbell or knocking on a door, but by walking into the house and announcing oneself. Hospitality was generous. A person arriving at mealtime was invited to stay and partake of what was available – the ultimate potluck guest. There were some who had well-deserved reputations for unerringly arriving in time for meals, sometimes after having ascertained the menu in advance from the domestic help. A person arriving other than at meal times, was bound to be offered, and required to partake, of some thing to eat and some refreshment. Second helpings were generally required, and refusal was considered insulting to the hosts.

Women ruled the household. In the middle class, employment outside the house was generally frowned upon for women. The selection of menus, the preparation and presentation of food was in their hands. They generally had household help. Meals were prepared on a wood fire, where the regulation of cooking temperatures was a particular art. More recently, gas and electric stoves and ovens have come into increasing use. Since refrigeration was not generally available, shopping was a daily chore and occupied a good portion of the morning at open-air markets. It was important to be there when items for sale were at their freshest. Fish, for example, were caught early in the morning and brought to market immediately in wicker baskets dripping with melting ice. Vendors also came to the door with fish, meat, eggs, milk, butter and vegetables. These supplemented homegrown produce in individual backyards (*quintais*) or garden patches. Poultry and pigs were also kept in backyards, and there was generally a supply of fresh eggs. Fish and meat had to be properly cleaned before cooking.

## Meals

Food production in the household was a continuous process. Extended families were large and there were four meals a day. Breakfast was around 9.00 am; lunch at about 1.30 pm; tea at 5.30 pm; and dinner at 8.30 pm. Lunch was the principal meal of the day, and was followed by a siesta, of about two hours, in the peak of the day's heat. Tea was followed by a period of socializing with family and friends. Before dinner, the family assembled on a verandah or *balcão* to take advantage of the cooler temperatures, before going in to dinner. Bedtime was between 10.30 pm and 11.00 pm.

Breakfast was some combination of *congee* (or *canja,* a rice broth), served with condensed curry, and tender mango pickled in salt water with spices (*chepniche amblim*), eggs in any form, toast, butter, mango jam, or guava jelly. Lunch was the principal meal: a light soup, rice and a curry dish, pickled fish and a variety of condiments and accompaniments, dessert or fruit. Dinner was a lighter meal with soup, a fish or meat dish, and fruit or dessert. Tea was a meal: tea was accompanied with *merenda* which could be sweet preparations of coconut and *jaggery* or various kinds of cookies, biscuits, and cakes.

Meals on special occasions (birthdays, wedding anniversaries, arrival of distinguished guests, or feast days), were usually in the middle of the day. They were something else altogether. The table groaned with food to justify the occasion. Some dishes appeared unfailingly: *xacuti, arroz refugado, sarapatel, apa de camarão, chouriço, bebinca,* and *alétria.* These strange sounding names describe dishes that have exotic combinations of spices and ingredients. They reflect the historical and cultural influences to which Goa has been exposed. The alcohols consumed also reflect these influences. Women drank as an *aperitif* a sweet Portuguese port or muscatel wine. Men drank scotch whiskey. During the meal Portuguese rosé or white (*granjo*) and red (*tinto*) wines were served. The meal concluded with brandy, cashew or palm *feni* (a local *eau de vie*). All this established ideal conditions for a prolonged siesta.

## Historical Perspective

The Portuguese arrived in Goa in the early 16th century when they were at the height of their maritime powers. The early Portuguese explorers, Vasco da Gama and Afonso de Albuquerque are intimately associated with Goa's colonial history. Afonso de Albuquerque, Governor of the Portuguese State in the East, attacked and captured Goa in March 1510 from Adil Shah, the ruler of the adjoining Indian State of Bijapur. Further conquests continued with the annexation of Bardez, Salcete, and Tiswadi (Ilhas) that constituted the *Velhas Conquistas* or Old Conquests. In 1781-88, the territory of Goa was further increased by the annexation of a significant amount of additional land of the *Novas Conquistas* or New Conquests. This became the territory of Goa as we know it today. On December 19, 1961, Goa was integrated with the rest of India, and today it is an Indian state.

Goan history, however, antedates Portuguese colonization by many centuries. There are references to Goa in the writings of the ancient Greeks and Romans, and in Hindu mythology. Even the name of the land seems to have multiple interpretations. In Sanskrit Aryan literature, Goa is claimed to mean "the country of cows". In pre-Aryan references, Goa is translated as "the land of the inclined paddy." Diogo de Couto referred to Goa as a "fertile and refreshing land." The *Kadamba* rulers of Goa from the 10$^{th}$ to the 14$^{th}$ century claimed that Goa was "the abode of welfare." It will become obvious, that these were attempts to define the name of the land, Goa, with qualities it possessed.

The history of Goa is driven by the attractiveness of its prime harbor, and its commercial importance in the *entrepot* trade. There is a relatively limited historical record of Goa up to the third century A.D. It is assumed that at that time the *Bhojas* ruled Goa up to the second century when another kingdom, the *Satavahanas*, exercised suzerainty of Goa. This was followed in the fifth century by what came to be known as the *Konkan Maurya* kingdom, an offshoot of the Hindu emperors who ruled most of northern India from their capital in Indore. Then in succession Goa was ruled by other Hindu dynasties – the *Rashtrakutas*, the *Chalukyas*, and the *Silaharas* - until the tenth century when they were replaced by yet another Hindu dynasty, the *Kadambas*, who controlled Goa from the 10$^{th}$ to the 14$^{th}$ centuries. In about 1320, Muslim conquerors linked with the *Mughal* emperors who ruled most of northern India defeated the *Kadambas* and took control of Goa. During the 14$^{th}$ century, the power of the *Kadambas* declined. The Muslim conquerors exercised only sporadic interest in Goa. Sovereignty over Goa was intermittently held by the kingdoms of the *Bahmanis* and of *Vijayanagar*. In 1472 the *Bahmanis* had control of Goa. But by 1489 they had to cede control to the Adil Shah kingdom of Bijapur. In March of 1510, the Portuguese under Afonso de Albuquerque, attacked and captured Goa, and thus established a Portuguese colonial empire in India, which lasted until 1961.

This rapid journey through almost twenty centuries of Goa's history provides scarce knowledge of the forces that influenced Goan cooking. In order to understand these forces, it is important to explore further the interaction between political developments and the external trade of Goa.

Due to accidents of geography and history and political developments, Goa is located at the principal trade routes between East Asia, India and the Arab world. Its location in the middle of the West Coast of India also placed it centrally in a thriving coastal trade. The Portuguese made Goa the capital of its *Estado da India* (or Indian State). This effectively covered not only the Portuguese territories in India, but also its possessions in the Far East (importantly Timor and Macao) and the eastern African territories. Goa was also used by Portuguese traders as a link in their trade between Portugal, Africa, and Brazil.

In the 16$^{th}$ century, according to the Portuguese historian Cabral e Sa, merchants found in Goa belonged to diverse religious groups and nations. They were Jews, Hindus, Christians, Jains and Muslims, from Persia, Arabia, Abyssinia, Portugal, Italy, Germany, and from other parts of India

– Gujarat, Kanara, and the Malabar Coast. Coins of various origins also circulated in Goa – *larins*, *pagodas*, *santhomes*, *pardãos*, *bazarucos*, *tangas*, *xerafins, venezians*, and *rials.*

This international presence reflected the importance of Goa in international trade in the 16th century. Goa was central in the *entrepot* trade. Goods and people came to Goa from different parts of India as well as from various parts of the world. From Muscat and Bahrain in the Arabian Peninsula came seed pearls, in exchange for ivory, coconuts, pepper, cloves, cinnamon, and cardamom, which had been brought to Goa from other parts of India and Ceylon (Sri Lanka). Textiles came to Goa from the kingdom of Gujarat in western India, and were exported to Mombassa and Mozambique in eastern Africa. Ships also carried goods to Goa from the Philippines, China, and (cloves from) Malacca. A small number of African slaves were brought to Goa and sold there for use in the plantations of Brazil. Goa exported to Brazil textiles from other parts of India, and imported tobacco, jams, sugar and ginger. There was in Goa in this period, also an active trade in Arabian horses, and trade in opium with Macao. Curiously, Goa was dependent on the surrounding parts of India for its daily food requirements of rice, oil, milk, eggs, fruits, and spices. As this commerce flourished, it brought in its wake the development of guilds of artisans and craftsmen, and classes of brokers and middlemen who were important in trade. Goa was very prosperous in the 16th century. This commerce also led to a major infusion of different kinds of food and spices which continue to this day to be such an integral part of Goan cuisine.

In 1628 the Portuguese East India Company was formed, but it collapsed in 1633. In the 17th century, the Dutch and the British challenged Portugal's hegemony of the sea routes to India and the Orient. As Portugal's power waned, there was a massive decline in Goa's trade. As historian M. N. Pearson has put it: "…Goa's vicissitudes in the seventeenth century were in large part a result of a change in the focus of empire. India was ignored; Brazil received all the attention and the resources. Godinho characterizes the Portuguese Empire in the fifteenth century as dominated by west African gold, the sixteenth by Asian pepper, and the seventeenth by Brazilian sugar. Brazil boomed as India stagnated…"

Initially, the Dutch challenged Portuguese dominance in the Asian trade through competition. As the 17th century wore on, however, the challenge took a military form, with attacks on their ships and sea-lanes. Between 1655 and 1663 the Dutch drove the Portuguese from Malabar, Macassar and Ceylon (Sri Lanka). The Dutch between 1638 and 1644, and again in 1656 to 1663, subjected Goa to yearly blockades. The Portuguese also faced other attacks both on sea and land. The Imams of Oman attacked the Portuguese and took control of the trade with the Arabian Peninsula. The Omanis also cut off the Portuguese eastern African trade. On land, the Marathas occupied Goa from 1737 to 1740. Although they were subsequently forced to withdraw, the northern part of the Portuguese territory, in particular the important area of Bassein was lost. On December 31, 1600 a royal charter created the British East India Company. Aware of Portuguese successes in Asia and of the riches of the trade in the area, the company attempted to found a factory in India. As is true of other colonial episodes of the period, commerce and trade was followed by the flag and military force. As economic historian Celsa Pinto has put it: "A review of the eighteenth and nineteenth centuries trading system of Goa has revealed that its destinies were intimately bound with and subordinated to British interests in India and the rest of the world, and was therefore linked with the European-based world economy in which England enjoyed the hegemonic core."

Indian textiles were at the core of Goa's export trade. The British glutted the Goan market with cheap machine-made British goods, which adversely affected Goa's trade. As the British developed Bombay, about 350 miles north of Goa, into a major commercial and trading center, Goa's coastal trade focused on Bombay. Goa's imports from Bombay exceeded its exports by a wide margin. Goa's merchants and traders became subordinate to those in Bombay. The Portuguese attempted to revitalize Goa's trade and to re-establish prosperity in Goa. They signed the Anglo-Portuguese treaty of 1878, establishing a rail link between Goa and British India. Since the British controlled the monopoly on salt, one of the principal exports from Goa, the treaty had the perverse effect of pushing the Goan economy further into the doldrums.

India became independent of Britain in 1947. Goa however continued as a Portuguese colony. In the 1950's, for political reasons, an economic blockade of Goa was put into place. This coincided with the exploitation and exports of Goan manganese and iron ore to Japan and other parts of the world. A new age of economic prosperity ensued. It was fueled by mineral exports and remittances by Goans working outside Goa. There was then a flood of imports from all over the world. From Europe came Portuguese wines and hard liquors, and all kinds of consumer goods (watches, cameras, European textiles and clothing, and other consumer durables). At the end of the colonial period in 1961, the standard of living of the average Goan was decidedly better than that of the average Indian. Income was more evenly distributed in Goa than in India. There were no indications of widespread poverty and malnutrition. By and large, rural houses in Goa were better than those in other parts of India. The villagers were better fed and clad. Even if this was the story at the end of colonialism, for some of the preceding centuries, the distribution of assets – land – was heavily concentrated. There were landlords (*batcaras*) with large land holdings, where tenants (*mundcares*) tilled the soil. The rich returns from these activities and from commerce saw the creation of large wealth and splendid houses with richly appointed furnishings that still exist in Goa and have recently been referred to as the *Palacios de Goa* (or Palaces of Goa). The architecture is an eclectic combination of East and West, as are many other aspects of Goan life. The beautiful churches and temples, the architectural style of houses, the placid qualities of rural life, and the tranquility of social interactions with established and extended families, communities (*communidades*), all gave a special quality and charm to life in Goa.

It is these qualities on which memories are based. This is also the context for this book of Goan recipes, which is one expression of this period in Goan history and culture.

## A View of the Influences on Goan Cuisine

There is no written record of the origins of individual Goan dishes. Sea routes were the transmission belts for culinary exchanges. Movements of humans from and to Goa carried the recipes and the ingredients over the ages. Goa was on the main trading routes between Asia, Africa, Europe, the Arab world, and Portuguese South America (Brazil). Goan cuisine absorbed, modified and made its own these diverse influences. The mark of a vital and exciting cuisine is its ability to do so. It was an historical accident that a coastal enclave came under colonial influence. It remained, for four centuries, on major trade routes at the intersection of important culinary exchanges. Ultimately, it was the Goan culinary genius that modified them and made them attractive to be re-exported, by its own people and visitors, to various parts of the world. We explore, with a measure of literary license, the influences on some traditional Goan dishes.

There is no dish that Goans consider more uniquely their own than *sarapatel* (see recipe in the Meat and Poultry section.) This spicy pork stew is a central feature of any festive meal. It is generally served with *sannas* (see recipe in the Rice and Bread section), a rice cake with a sweetish taste that balances the pungency of the *sarapatel.* Therefore, it comes as a great surprise to a Goan to discover that the cuisine of Bahia, in the northeast of Brazil, also includes a dish called *sarapatel.* Could this dish have evolved in two places at the same time? Or, did it come from a common origin that was neither Goa nor Brazil? Or, was it taken by the Portuguese from one place to another, and if so, from where to where? Goa, Bahia, and the west coast of Africa have some common elements. They have similar agro-ecological conditions and climate - recall that prior to the period of the Continental Drift, the northeast of Brazil (Bahia) and the west coast of Africa were physically united. Some of the same crops and spices could therefore be grown in all three places. Further, Africans were part of the mercenary forces included in the Portuguese army in Goa, and were taken as slaves to work on the sugarcane plantations of northeast Brazil. Could the common link then be African cuisine? But, in the 16th century, Islam was the dominant religion on the west coast of Africa, and it forbids the eating of pork. It thus seems unlikely that *sarapatel* could have been taken to Goa and Bahia from Africa. More likely, it either originated in Goa and was taken by the Portuguese to Bahia, or the other way around. The Brazilian author Darwin Brandão's *A Cozinha Baiana* is considered to be one of the classic books on the cooking of Bahia. In examining Baiana cooking he remarks that: "a presenca do portugues aparece aqui e ali. Aparece no sarapatel que os colonizadores trouxeram da India…." (the Portuguese presence appears here and there. It appears in sarapatel which the colonizers brought from India.) *Sarapatel* is consumed in Bahia to this day. It probably reflects the christianization of the population and the dissipation of the taboo on the preparation and consumption of pork.

In Goa, *sarapatel* is generally eaten with *sannas,* a kind of spongy rice cake that is cooked in a special double steamer, in a manner similar to Chinese *dim sum*. *Sannas* are similar to the *idlis* of southern Indian cooking. They, however, differ from them in one important respect, the use of *sura* or palm toddy as a leavening ingredient in their preparation, that gives a certain zing to *sannas*. The combination of the spicy taste of *sarapatel* is balanced by the sweetish aromatic *sannas*. An irresistible combination!

A few other brief examples will suffice to illustrate the variety of influences on Goan cooking. *Xacuti (*a kind of stew) is another typically Goan dish. The classic recipe for this dish requires the use of goat meat, and is, in all likelihood derived from Muslim cooking. In modern times, mutton, chicken, or wild game are used (see recipe in the Meat and Poultry section.) There are two unusual aspects of this dish. It utilizes grated coconut as a central element of the dish both to stanch the otherwise pungent combination of spices, and also to thicken the sauce. This thickening of the sauce is required because *xacuti* is generally eaten with *oddes*. These are the *puris*, or rice flour puffs, used in southern Indian cooking. While *puris* are eaten with vegetarian dishes in southern Indian cooking, in Goan cooking they are eaten with a meat dish. An example of the blending of two different cuisines.

The mix of cuisines also shows up in the preparation of seafood. Mackerels are stuffed *(peixe recheado)* with a blended paste combination (*mirem*) of garlic, peppercorns, chilies, turmeric, cumin seeds, coriander seeds, ginger, tamarind, salt and vinegar. The fish is then either fried or baked and served as an accompaniment to a rice dish. This fish preparation is a deliciously spicy version of stuffed fish dishes found in southern European cuisine, with spices taking the place of tasty but blander mixtures of shrimp, herbs and sauces.

The most typically Goan daily curry dish, however, is a shrimp curry that is served with steamed white rice (*xitt koddi*). The shrimp is cooked in a curry made with onions, ginger, garlic, ground cumin seeds, turmeric, red chilies, and coconut milk. This is the Goan version of a prawn stew found in Iberian and Latin American cuisine. It is distinguished not so much by the use of spices (which can be found in East Asian cuisine), but by the use of coconut milk. The use of coconut in a variety of dishes, from soup to main courses to desserts, probably stems from the ready availability of this nut all over the land. Coconut has become a distinguishing feature of Goan cuisine.

A Goan rice dish that is featured in most festive meals is *arroz refugado*. This is clearly of Iberian origin, familiar as a dish with the same name in Portugal and *paella* in Spain. The Iberian versions include saffron, which gives the rice its yellow color. This expensive spice is not indigenous to that part of the world, and must have been brought there by Arab traders either from Iran, Turkey or Kashmir, where it is indigenous. The Goan version of this dish includes shrimp and spicy *chouriço*, garnished with green olives (*azeitonas*) of Portuguese or Mediterranean origin. This is a dish that incorporates a spice native to India, which then finds its way back to Goa.

An interesting twist on the cross-cultural influences on Goan cooking is *balchão*, which generally accompanies a rice dish. *Balchão* is a shrimp dish that uses a pungent dry shrimp paste and, in the Goan version, also incorporates *bilimbim*, a sour vegetable that is a relative of the French *cornichon*. According to Wendy Hutton, in an article entitled *East Meets West in the Kitchen* published in the December 1997 issue of *Going Places*, *balchão* was brought to Goa from Malacca (Malaysia) by the Malaccan brides of Portuguese men who went to both Goa and Macao. Evidently, a form of dried shrimp paste known as *balichão* is made in a few fishing villages in southern China, just across the border from Macao. This shrimp paste is only used in dishes in Macao, and is not found in Chinese cooking. In Goan cooking, the *bilimbim* has been added to the shrimp and spices to give it a local flavor.

Goan desserts, as those in the rest of India, tend to be rather rich and sweet. Ask a Goan to name a traditional and much loved dessert, and the answer will infallibly be *bebinca*. *Bebinca* is the dessert *de rigueur* for any festive meal. It is made from an extravagant number of egg yolks, combined with wheat flour, coconut milk, sugar, nutmeg and vanilla. This dessert has the consistency of *flan* or *crème caramel*. It is in the form of a cake of many thin layers that are baked one on top of the other, and there are thin brown lines of caramelized sugar separating the layers. It is an extremely rich dish, and its preparation is very time consuming because the layers have to be baked sequentially, while assuring that the preceding layers do not burn. This meticulous attention to its preparation indicates a cook's desire to honor the guests at the meal. The origin of this dish, as is also true of many other Goan dishes, is not known. It does seem that it might have originated with a religious order of nuns in a convent in Old Goa, who prepared this and other dessert dishes for sale to raise revenues. It is contended that they replaced milk, which is used in the preparation of *flan* and *crème caramel*, and which is in very short supply in Goa, with coconut milk. This is probably a dish of Iberian origin. In the Philippines, which was colonized by Spain and which also has trade links with Malacca (Malaysia), there is a dessert that is also called *bebingka*. It is made of mashed bananas, and is also cooked in layers. In Sierra Leone it is made of cassava. The Goan *bebinca* is not recommended for those who are watching their cholesterol levels. However, even for them, the taste of a thin sliver of this wickedly delicious dessert is recommended as an essential part of the introduction to Goan cooking.

Another dessert that shows a blend of Portuguese influence on Goan cooking is *alétria*. As its base, this dish uses grated fresh coconut that is cooked in sugar syrup, and decorated with fine threads of egg yolk, also cooked in syrup, and either almonds or cashew nuts. The recipe for this dish, blending Goan and Portuguese influences is also attributed to the same religious order of nuns who, it is claimed gave *bebinca* to Goan cooking.

We end here this preliminary excursion into the rich and complex cross-cultural influences on Goan cuisine. The lack of written materials constrains the depth to which one can go in authenticating the ideas presented above. But the oral tradition is very powerful in Goa. Perhaps readers could bring additional insights to what seems to be an interesting story embedded in Goan dishes and cooking.

**References**

This chapter has drawn on a variety of sources. Principal among these are:

1. Brandão, Darwin, *A Cozinha Baiana*, 2nd ed., Editora Letras e Artes, Rio de Janeiro, 1965.
2. Carita, Helder, *Palacios de Goa*, Quetzal Editores, 2nd ed., Lisboa, 1966.
3. da Fonseca, Jose Nicolau, *Historical and Archaeological Sketch of the City of Goa*, Thacker & Co. Ltd., Bombay, 1878
4. de Saldanha, M.J. Gabriel, *Historia de Goa*, 2 vols., Livraria Coelho, Nova Goa, 1925
5. de Souza, Teotonio R., *Medieval Goa: A Socio-Economic History*, Concept Publishing Company, New Delhi, 1979
6. de Souza, Teotonio R. (editor), *Goa through the Ages*, Volume II, Goa University Publishing Series No. 6, Concept Publishing Company, New Delhi, 1990
7. Gonçalves, Julio, *Os Portugueses E O Mar das Indias*, Livraria Luso-Espanhola, Lda., Lisboa, 1947

## II. SPICES IN GOAN COOKING

The trade in spices is historically a very old one and predates the colonial period. India had been at the center of the spice trade. The search for dominance of this trade is part of the history of the struggles between the colonial powers for maritime hegemony. This accounts for the establishment of the British East India Company, the French *Compagnie des Indes*, the Dutch East India Company, and the Portuguese *Companhia das Indias*. Goa was at the center of the Portuguese colonial and trading empire that covered the colonies in the Far East and Africa. The Dutch ceding Manhattan to the British in 1667 in exchange for the Indonesian Spice Islands (the island of Run which was the sole source of highly prized nutmeg at that time) evidences the mythical importance of spices in transactions between colonial powers.

A popular conception of Eastern cuisine is that it is heavily spiced to cover up the poor quality of the basic ingredients – vegetables, fish and meats – used in the cuisine. This ignores the potential dangers of ingesting spoiled and bacteria-infested foods. Contaminated food would be highly dangerous for poor people in weakened physical conditions. It seems more likely, as recent research seems to indicate, that spices were used, in countries with hot climates where unrefrigerated food spoils quickly, to prevent bacterial build-up in foods. The spices that strongly inhibit bacterial growth include chili peppers, garlic, onion, cinnamon, cumin, lemongrass, bay leaf, cloves and oregano. These spices appear with frequency in tropical recipes. There is also evidence that the spices used in each country were particularly effective against the local bacteria. And, that since meats are more susceptible to food-borne diseases than are vegetables, the former are cooked with more spices than are the latter. Further, the spices and herbs used are closely related to the bacteria found in the specific climatic zone. This applies to Western Hemisphere countries and those in the Tropics. The use of spices as preservatives is evident in the use of curing with salt and spices that characterized European and American cooking of the early 19th century before the availability of refrigeration. Today, the use of spices in quality Goan and other Asian cuisines is a matter of tradition, taste and habit, as it is in Western cuisine. There is, however, now an increasing recognition of the health benefits of certain spices that might in part also explain their use.

In ancient Greece and Rome spices were valued originally for their medicinal, aphrodisiac and prophylactic qualities, and only later for seasoning food and drink. Science frequently accompanied trade, with the continual search for new plants that had medicinal value. "The Portuguese physician Garcia de Orta (*Coloquios dos simples e drogas e cousas medicinais da India,*) worked in Goa, to discover the real origins of spices about which so many legends had been told: to match names and descriptions from Greek, Latin, Arabic and Aramaic medical books; to gather new knowledge of their dietary and medical effects from Indian colleagues." We explore below the medicinal value of individual spices.

*Preparation and availability of spices*: In preparing Goan dishes, as in most other cuisines, it is best to use fresh ingredients to the maximum extent possible. The spices used in Goan recipes are available either in fresh or ground form in Asian (Indian or Thai) grocery stores or in larger supermarket chains. The prices of spices are lower, and the variety larger, in Asian stores. Ground spices lose their flavor and potency if they are exposed to air. Spices should be stored carefully in tightly covered containers in a cool, dry place. In Goa, the preparation of spices is a time-consuming process. The spices are ground using a large piece of hard stone that is chipped to provide a rough surface, and the grinding is done with another cylindrical piece of stone – a

Goan version of the mortar and pestle. Fortunately, now the spices are available in ground form, making for more expeditious cooking. Also, spices can be mixed in advance (see the recipe for *mirem* in the "Useful Tips" section) and, if properly refrigerated and stored, can be used for preparing dishes in short order. Curried dishes can be frozen for future use. The taste of curries improves as a result of freezing as the seafood and meats are further marinated by the freezing process. Re-heating curried dishes in microwave ovens is not recommended.

Some selected spices commonly used in Goan cooking are discussed below, both to bring out their uses and their nutritional properties.

*Turmeric (haldi)*: India is the greatest source of supply of this spice. Turmeric is a root similar to ginger and thrives in a hot, humid, tropical climate. There are references in the Vedas and the Ramayana, dating back thousands of years, to the use of this spice for the coloring of rice. Turmeric has a peppery aroma and flavor. It has a rich yellow color. In Goan cooking, turmeric is used as a substitute for the very expensive saffron. It gives aroma and the yellow color to curries and pickles. Turmeric is a mild digestive and antiseptic and is used to alleviate liver complaints and stomach ulcers. It is used as a cure for colds by being boiled with milk. Its most desirable form is as a dried root that is ground for immediate use. It is available in a ground and powdered form that should be stored in a tightly sealed container.

*Saffron (kesar):* This is an extremely expensive spice. It takes 200,000 hand-picked flowers to make a single pound. Arab traders introduced saffron from the Near East to China, to India and to Spain, where some of the finest quality saffron is now grown. Saffron is also grown in Greece, Turkey, Iran, Morocco, and Kashmir. High quality saffron is available in orange-red threads of the stigmata of the flowers. Saffron has a distinctive warm flavor. Because it is very expensive it is used discriminatingly in Goan cooking, principally in desserts made of milk. Saffron is used as a sedative and anti-spasmodic. Although it does not have the flavor or taste of saffron, turmeric is used as a substitute for saffron in curries and rice dishes.

*Ginger (adrak):* The name of this spice purportedly has Sanskrit origins. Ginger is referred to in the writings of Confucius and is an integral element of Ayurvedic medicine for the relief of liver ailments, indigestion, coughs, colds, and anemia. Ginger originated either in India or China. Arab traders took it to ancient Greece and Rome and eastern Africa, and the Portuguese to western Africa. Ginger figures prominently in Goan curries and pickles, in diced, thinly sliced or chopped, or grated form. Ginger has a sharp, lemony taste. Preferably, it should be used in fresh rather than powdered form. Fresh ginger root is available in most grocery stores.

*Garlic (lehsun):* It features in the religion, culture, and mythology of many countries. It is also a common and indispensable part of many cuisines, including that of Goa. Garlic comes in bulbs that are made up of cloves. It is grown in many parts of the world, including India, China, the Middle East, Latin America and the United States. Garlic is thought to have strong medicinal properties. It purifies the blood and lowers blood pressure, aids digestion, is an aid in the treatment of diabetes, and it is used as a cough medicine. In cooking, it is important not to brown garlic, as it will then have a bitter taste. According to the recipe, garlic is either chopped finely, cut in flakes, minced or crushed. In Goan cuisine fresh garlic, which is available in most grocery stores, is used.

*Cumin (jeera)*: A native of the Nile Valley, cumin seeds have been found in the tombs of the Pharaohs. Presumably, Arab traders brought this spice to India and Goa. Cumin has a strong, aromatic, and spicy taste. It is used in a variety of cuisines. In seed form it is used in bread in France and Germany, and in cheeses in Holland and Switzerland. It is also used in Middle Eastern cooking, in *couscous*, lamb and meat dishes. Cumin seeds are generally fried for a few minutes in a heavy pan to bring out their aroma, before being used in either seed or ground form. In seed form, cumin is used in Goan meat, vegetable and rice dishes and pickles; in ground form it is used in seafood dishes. Cumin is an essential ingredient of most *masalas*. Cumin is considered as an appetite stimulant and also as a digestive aid. It is not uncommon to conclude an Indian meal by chewing on cumin seeds.

*Coriander /Cilantro (dhania)*: A part of the carrot and parsley family, it is native to the Mediterranean and the Middle East. Coriander is also grown extensively in India, Brazil and other parts of South America, Russia and Holland. Coriander is available in either seed form, or as fresh cilantro leaves. Seeds are best lightly roasted to bring out their aroma before being powdered. Large quantities of coriander are used in almost all Goan curried dishes, and in pickles and chutneys. Fresh cilantro leaves are used in soups and in steamed fish dishes as a garnish. Coriander seeds have antibacterial properties and their oil is used in the treatment of colic, neuralgia, and rheumatism.

*Chilies (mirchi)*: They are native to Mexico and were taken by Christopher Columbus to Europe, and from there to Africa, India, and the Far East. Chilies now constitute an essential element of cooking in most countries of the so-called developing world of Asia, Africa and North, Central and South America. The presumption is that all curries are pungent because they contain chilies. In fact, in many households, for dietary or other reasons, curries can have varying degrees of pungency. In Goan cooking, many curry dishes have attenuated the pungency of the use of chilies, through the use of coconut milk that has a sweetish taste. Chilies used in Goan cooking are either of the small red or green varieties, or what are known as the Kashmiri and Madrasi chilies that are larger in size. If a dish is too pungent for one's taste, an antidote is to eat boiled rice with it, rather than drinking water or an alcoholic beverage. Chilies are rich in Vitamin C, and they cool the body in hot climates by making the body sweat.

*Curry-Pak Leaves (meetha neem)*: These leaves come from a tree that is native to Southern India and Sri Lanka. They have a strong curry aroma. They are generally broken into fine pieces and added to curry dishes. They are also used in pickles, but in larger pieces. In Goan cooking they are also used in seafood dishes.

*Cloves (laung)*: The first recorded use of cloves is by the Chinese in the first century BC. Cloves are native to the Indonesian Spice Islands. They were the source of intense competition between the Dutch, French and British in the 18$^{th}$ century in the East Indies, until they were smuggled by Pierre Poivre and grown in Mauritius. Cloves are staple elements in Indian and Goan cooking. Whole cloves are used in broths to flavor fish. They are also used to give the particular aroma to Goan rice dishes, such as *arroz refugado*. Cloves, either in ground or whole form, are also used in the preparation of fruit and vegetable chutneys. It is the warm and pungent aroma of cloves that dictates their use. Cloves have strong antiseptic and preservative properties. The oil of cloves is used to treat colic, flatulence, indigestion and toothaches.

*Mustard seeds (rai):* Brown mustard seeds are indigenous to India and are grown throughout the country. They have a sharp, hot taste. The seeds are cooked in hot oil until they pop and are then added to vegetable or *dal* (lentil) dishes. It is advisable to use a splatter screen to prevent the mustard seeds from flying out of the pan during the popping stage. Mustard is added to baths to relieve muscular aches and pains. As a chest poultice it is used to relieve respiratory ailments.

*Poppy seeds* (*khas khas*) Arab traders introduced the poppy to Persia, India and South-East Asia. Indian poppy seeds are creamy colored and are used for thickening curries. They are also added to bread. The seeds are sweet smelling and have a nutty aroma when cooked. They are usually roasted in a pan before use. Poppy seeds are said to relieve toothache and earache.

*Tamarind: (imli)* The word "*tamarind*" means the date of India. In the Arab world, tamarind is known as *tamar hindi*. It is believed to be native to East Africa, and is now extensively grown in various parts of India. Tamarind has a sweet-sour fruity taste. It is available in most Indian and Thai grocery stores either as fresh tamarind pods, or compressed tamarind block, or as a concentrated tamarind powder. Tamarind is used in most Goan curry dishes and in chutneys and pickles. In its fresh form it consists of pods that have a shell. It has to be peeled to get to the fruit, which surrounds a hard, dark brown seed. When cooking with fresh tamarind, the shelled pod is soaked in hot water, and the liquid is then added to curries. When a compressed tamarind block is used, a piece is cut off, soaked in hot water, and the liquid is added to the curry. In concentrated powder form, tamarind is added directly to the liquid of a curry. Tamarind is claimed to have medicinal properties for stomach upsets and as a laxative.

*Fenugreek (methi):* It is native to India and Southern Europe. Fenugreek is highly aromatic and smells like curry. It has a tangy flavor. The leaves are generally used in the preparation of spinach and potato dishes, and the seeds are ground and used in curry masalas (*mirem*) for cooking fish and vegetables. In the Middle Ages, fenugreek was used as a cure for baldness. Now it is used for low blood pressure and anemia.

*Cinnamon (dalchini):* A spice native to Sri Lanka where it was cultivated by the Portuguese, Dutch and British East India Company, it spread to the Seychelles, Jamaica and Brazil (recall Jorge Amado's famous novel *Gabriela, Cravo e Canela.*) Cinnamon has a sweet and warm fragrance. The rolled cinnamon sticks that are available in grocery stores are the bark of the cinnamon tree, a bushy evergreen tree of the laurel family. Cinnamon is one of the prime ingredients of *garam masala* and is used to flavor rice dishes, and desserts, and as a spice for tea. It is used as an antidote for diarrhea and stomach upsets.

*Cardamom (ilaichi):* There are references to the use of cardamom in Indian Ayurvedic medicine as early as 4 BC. In India, cardamom is referred to as the "Queen of Spices". It was introduced to Western Europe by the early spice traders, and was much prized by the ancient Romans. Cardamom is hand-picked and hence is a relatively expensive spice. Cardamom has a mellow lemon and camphor smell, contained in the seeds inside pods. Cardamom comes in three colors – green, black and white. It is used in Goan rice dishes, sweets and desserts. Cardamom is used as a breath freshener and as an aid to digestion.

*Nutmeg (jaifal):* Known for its curative properties, nutmeg is used in ayurvedic medicine for headaches and fevers. Pierre Poivre transported it from the Indonesian Spice Islands to Mauritius and broke the Dutch monopoly on the trade in this spice. Nutmeg has a strong aromatic smell. It is best to buy the whole nutmeg nuts and to grate them for use. Nutmeg is used as a flavoring in cakes, puddings, pies, and other desserts.

*Vanilla*: Native to Mexico, it was cultivated by the Aztecs. In the 16th century, the Spanish conquerors took vanilla to the West and it spread from there to the rest of the world. The Portuguese brought vanilla to Goa. It is available as a bean or in the form of an extract of vanilla. Vanilla is a very delicate flavor that is used in sweets, and in particular with chocolate. In Goan cuisine it is used in desserts that are of Portuguese origin. Although there are medicinal benefits claimed for vanilla, there is no evidence of direct benefits, except psychological.

**Concluding comment**: A Goan kitchen has this wide range of spices. They are combined as needed to provide the different flavors appropriate to the fish, crustacean, meat or vegetable that is being prepared. Pungency can also be controlled by the combination of ingredients, as can the other flavors. The combination of spices also leads to alluring aromas and combinations of colors that entice the diner to the table.

## COCONUT

Goa is known as the producer of delicious mangoes of different varieties (the best known is the *Afonso* or *Alphonso* mango), and the humbler coconut. The coconut palm (*cocos nucifera*) can be seen everywhere in Goa. It grows in all kinds of soil, including the sandy variety. Coconut trees border roads, define property boundaries, grow on the embankments of paddy fields, and provide shade at the edges of rivers and on beaches.

Coconut trees and their products are an integral part of Goan life and cooking. Coconuts have four parts: a green outer husk, which covers a hard brown shell, which is lined with a white pulp, which contains water. All these parts are used in Goan cooking. The dried husks and shells serve as cooking fuel. The husk is also shredded into coir and made into welcome mats. The pulp is grated and used to make coconut milk, or used directly in meat dishes and cakes and other desserts. Two noteworthy desserts made with coconut are *"Teias de Aranha"* or *Spider's Webs*, and *Pinaca*. [See recipes in the Dessert section]. The former calls for the use of thin slivers of tender (early development) coconut cooked in syrup. *Pinaca* is a sweet snack. Other uses of coconut extracts are: the coconut water is drunk as an aid to digestion and to boost the immune system; the sap of the coconut palm is fermented and made into *feni*, a potent *eau de vie,* or into vinegar that is used for cooking. Fronds of the coconut palm are dried and braided together to shelter the mud walls and the roofs of modest village houses against the torrential Goan monsoons.

Coconuts are harvested every year in May. Men climb the swaying trunks of coconut palms with amazing agility. Armed with a sharp long bladed knife, the coconuts are cut loose from their branches and drop to the ground in bunches. They are then counted and apportioned between the landowner and the tenant farmer. Traditionally, they were transported to the landowner's house or to market in a bullock cart. Landowners stored coconuts in pantry sheds for home consumption. Coconuts for market are shelled, cracked open and dried in the sweltering hot May sun until the dried coconut pulp (or *copra*) readily separates from the shell. The *copra* is transported to a mill where it is pressed into coconut oil, which is used for cooking or to revitalize women's hair. The residue is made into *jaggery,* a brown coarse sugar that is used for sweets and desserts.

**References**

1. Clevely, Andi; Richmond, Katherine; Morris, Sallie and Mackley, Lesley, *The Encyclopedia of Herbs and Spices*, Ammess Publishing Ltd., New York, 1997
2. Dalby, Andrew, *Dangerous Tastes*: The Story of Spices, the University of California Press, 2000
3. Garcia de Orta, *Coloquios dos simples e drogas e cousas medicinais de India*, printed in Goa in 1563
4. Kiple, Kenneth F. and Conèe Ornelas, Kriemhild, (editors), *The Cambridge World of History of Food*, Vol. I and II, Cambridge University Press, 2000
5. Milton, Giles, *Nathaniel's Nutmeg*, Penguin USA, 2000
6. Sherman, Paul W. and Flaxman, Samuel, Protecting *Ourselves from Food*, American Scientist, Vol. 89, March-April, 2001, pp. 142-146
7. Wild, Anthony, *The East India Company Book of Spices*, Harper-Collins Publishers, London, 1995

# III.  USEFUL TIPS

The recipes included in this book call for the use of *grated coconut, coconut milk,* and a *coconut curry base.* Unsweetened *grated coconut* is available in Indian and Thai grocery stores. Tins of *coconut milk* (again unsweetened) are also available in these stores. Coconut milk can also be made out of *coconut cream*, sliced and soaked in hot water, available in packages in the freezer section of these stores. *Coconut curry base* consists of grated coconut mixed with appropriate spices called for in the individual recipes.

The traditional way of making these forms of coconut products is described below. Cooking implements required include: a heavy cleaver, a cheese cloth, a grater (available in Indian and Thai grocery stores), a mortar and pestle or a blender (in Goa, a flat heavily rough textured piece of stone along with a round roughly textured stone is traditionally used.)

**Grated coconut**

*Ingredient*: 1 coconut with outer husk removed

*Preparation*
1. Pierce the two eyes at the top of the coconut with a screwdriver or other pointed object. Drain and keep the water in a drinking glass in the refrigerator for future consumption.
2. Using a heavy cleaver, crack the coconut along its middle into two halves.
3. Clamp the grater onto a kitchen counter. Position the half shell on the grater and turn the handle vigorously until the pulp is grated.
    *Caution*: do not allow any of the brown shell to mix with the grated pulp.
4. Grate the other half coconut. The result is a grated coconut. It can be stored in plastic containers in the freezer section of a refrigerator and thawed out for use as needed.

**Coconut milk**

*Ingredient*: 1 grated coconut

*Preparation*
1. Place the grated coconut in the cavity of a large mortar and pestle, or in a blender.
2. Add 1 cup to 1 ½ cups of cold water and grind or blend.
3. Squeeze the mixture through a cheesecloth or fine strainer.
4. This first extraction is called "thick coconut milk".
5. Repeat steps 2 and 3. The result is a second extraction of "thin coconut milk."
6. The coconut milk can be stored in plastic containers in the freezer section of a refrigerator, and thawed out for use as needed.

**Mirem or *Masala* /Ground paste**

One combination of spices that is commonly used in Goan cooking is "*mirem*"or "*masala*". This can be prepared in advance, and stored in an air-tight container, in the refrigerator for several months.  It is used particularly in meat-based recipes but also in some fish dishes. This recipe includes ginger although this tradition which was not universally followed.

*Ingredients*

Water to soak tamarind
1 tablespoon tamarind without seeds
12 Kashmiri chilies
1 teaspoon turmeric powder
8 cloves of garlic
1 inch piece of ginger (optional)
½ tablespoon of coriander seeds
1 teaspoon of cumin seeds
1 tablespoon of white vinegar
1 teaspoon salt (if needed)

**Mirem or Masala / Ground paste**

*Preparation*
1. Soak the tamarind in a little water and extract the pulp (see below under "Tamarind Juice").
2. Grind all the ingredients with the vinegar (if necessary for consistency, add a little bit of vinegar) in the blender.
3. If desired, you can add 1 teaspoon of salt.
4. Put paste in a jar tightly sealed and refrigerate. Use as needed. Can be kept for 3 to 6 months.

## Garlic-Ginger Paste

*Ingredients:*

*For the Garlic paste*
2 tablespoon of water
6 cloves of garlic

*For the Ginger paste*
1- 2 tablespoons of water
1 inch piece of fresh ginger

*Preparation*
1. Put the ingredients in a blender and make into a smooth paste.

*Note:* You may make a larger quantity, proportionately, of the garlic and ginger paste. Use only what is needed and store the rest in the refrigerator, for future use. It will keep for two weeks.

**Tamarind Juice**

To prepare tamarind juice, one has to use the pulp of the dried fruit. Tamarind is available in Indian stores in 1- lb cakes.

*Ingredients*

1 cup tamarind pulp
2 cups hot water

*Preparation*
1. Soak the tamarind pulp in the hot water for approximately 2 hours.
2. Put the mixture through a fine sieve. Add another tablespoon of hot water if necessary.
3. Store the tamarind water in a jar for future use.

## IV. Goan Recipes

## A. Soups and Appetizers

### Soups

Basic Chicken Stock
Basic Beef Stock
*Canja/Pez* (Rice Soup)
*Canja de Galinha* (Chicken and Rice Soup)
*Caldo Verde* (Green Soup)
Coriander Leaf (Cilantro) Soup
Coriander Leaf (Cilantro) and Green Pea Soup
Cucumber Soup I
Cucumber Soup II
Vegetable Soup
Asparagus Soup
*Dal* (Lentil) Soup
*Sopa de Camarão* (Prawn Soup)
Bacon Soup

### Appetizers

*Rissoes de Camarão* (Prawn Puffs)
*Fofos de Peixe* (Fish Rolls)
*Empadinhas* (Small Pork Pies)
*Fofos de Queijo* (Cheese Puffs)
Shrimp Toast
*Forminhas* (Tartlets)
Meat Patties

## A. Soups and Appetizers

### Soups

Soups are basically an influence of the Western world on the eating habits of Goans. The only native soup, if it can be so designated, is *congee* (*canja* in Portuguese and *pez* in the local dialect, Konkani). It is truly peasant food, heavy on the stomach and nutritious at the same time, as it consists entirely of unpolished rice cooked to the desired softness in water, to which a modicum of salt is added. It is cooked in an earthernware vessel and served out of the same with a coconut-shell ladle.

Even today one is likely to see women in rural areas, poising the vessel on their heads or balancing it on their hip, as they take it to their men at work in the fields. *Congee* is often used as a cure for dehydration in gastro-intestinal disorders.

In affluent families, *congee* becomes part of the morning breakfast or sometimes a mid-morning snack. However, once it appears on the master's table, it is served in all likelihood in a blue-and-white China export tureen, with a china ladle, and accompanied by a series of tasty tidbits such as vegetable pickles, pickled fish, or leftover condensed curry. On festive occasions, such as weddings, a "*canja de galinha*" (chicken *congee*) makes its appearance – the finest long-grain rice is used, cooked in chicken broth, flavored with bits of Portuguese sausage and green olives – almost a meal in itself.

Soup is always the first course of a meal in middle and upper class Goan families. The recipes here show the use of local or imported vegetables in the making of soup, and we start the section with two basic broth recipes which are the basis for a number of soups as well as of other dishes. Hence, we recommend that, when convenient, the cook prepare these broths, and freeze them, if necessary, for future use.

### Basic Chicken Stock

*Ingredients*

Preparation time: 30 minutes
Cooking time: 2 hours

1 3-lb chicken, skinned, cleaned and cut into pieces
8 cups water
2 medium-size white onions chopped into quarters
4 bay leaves
8 whole cloves of garlic, peeled
8 whole peppercorns
2 teaspoons salt

*Preparation*
1. Put all the listed ingredients in a large pot and cook over medium heat, covered, until it comes to a boil.
2. Reduce the heat to low and cook covered for 1 ½ to 2 hours, until the liquid is reduced to approximately 6 cups.

3. With a slotted spoon, remove chicken pieces. Separate the meat from the bones and save for future use.
4. Strain the soup through a fine mesh strainer. If not used immediately, it may be refrigerated for up to two days or frozen for up to 3 months.

*Note:* This stock and the chicken pieces are used for soup, *congee, arroz refugado* (flavored rice), or *arroz arabe*, to mention a few dishes. As a substitute for this stock you may dissolve 1 to 1 ½ cubes of chicken bouillon (depending on the size of the cube) in 1 cup of boiling water, or use a corresponding amount of canned chicken stock.

## Beef Stock

*Ingredients*
(For about 2 ½ quarts of stock)

Preparation time: 30 minutes
Cooking time: 3 hours

1 ½ lb of beef bones and trimmings
½ lb of chuck beef, cut into cubes
3 carrots, peeled and sliced into rounds
1 large onion, cut into quarters
1 turnip, cut into cubes
3 quarts hot water
1 tablespoon salt

*Preparation:*
1. In a saucepan, on medium high heat, place the beef bones and meat and allow them to brown in their own fat.
2. Toss in the carrots, onion and turnip and let them cook 2 minutes. Immediately, add the hot water and the salt. Bring to a boil.
3. Lower the heat to allow the mixture *to simmer* for about 3 hours.
4. Strain through a fine mesh strainer. Place the broth in the refrigerator.
5. When thoroughly chilled, remove the fat that accumulates on the surface.
6. If not used immediately, freeze for later use.

*Note:* This stock and the pieces of meat can be used in several soups and rice dishes. As a substitute for this stock you may dissolve 1 or 1 ½ beef bouillon cubes (depending on the size of the cube) in 1 cup of boiling water or use the measured amount of canned beef bouillon, if available.

## *Canja/Pez*
(Rice Soup)

*Ingredients* (4 servings)

Preparation time: 20 minutes
Cooking time: 20 minutes

½ cup rice (preferably brown rice, but other varieties may be used)
3 cups of water
½ to 1 teaspoon of salt

*Preparation:*
1. Wash the rice two or three times in cold water, or until the water runs clear. Drain.
2. In a saucepan, place the 3 cups of water with the salt, and then add the washed rice.
3. Cook on medium heat until rice grains are soft (approximately 20 minutes depending on the kind of rice used--brown rice takes longer to cook).
4. Serve in soup bowls with spicy tidbits (mentioned in the introduction to the "Soup" section).

## *Canja de Galinha*
(Chicken and Rice Soup)

*Ingredients* (4 servings)

Preparation time: 15 minutes
Cooking time: 20 minutes

4 cups of chicken stock (see recipe above)
¼ cup long-grain or Basmati rice (washed and drained)
1 cup chicken meat, cut into small pieces (see chicken stock recipe above)
Salt to taste
1- 6 inch Portuguese sausage, mild, medium or hot, sliced into thin rounds
¼ cup green olives

*Preparation:*
1. Put all listed ingredients (except olives and 4 sausage slices) in a large pot and cook over low heat till rice is soft (approximately 20-25 minutes).
2. Place in soup bowls, garnish with one or two olives and a sausage slice. This soup must be served very hot.

## *Caldo Verde*
(Green Soup)

This is the signature soup of Portugal, made with the produce grown in a homeowner's vegetable patch.

*Ingredients* (4 servings)  Preparation time: 30 minutes
Cooking time: 15 minutes

¾ cup Portuguese rapini or Swiss chard (the original recipe calls for "*couve galega*")
3 tablespoons olive oil
2 medium potatoes, cut into cubes
6 cups of chicken stock
Salt to taste
Black pepper to taste
½ of a 6 inch Portuguese sausage cut into thin rounds

*Preparation*
1. Wash and cut rapini or chard in very thin strips. Set aside.
2. In a saucepan, place the oil, the cubed potatoes, the chicken stock, the salt and pepper. Cook over medium heat until the potatoes are soft.
3. Remove from heat, place the mixture in a blender and blend for one or two minutes, until there are no lumps in the mixture.
4. Return the mixture to the pan, and bring it to a gentle boil. Immediately throw in the shredded greens and the sausage rounds, and allow them to cook for about 10 minutes, uncovered, so that the greens retain their color. Serve piping hot.

## Coriander Leaf (Cilantro) Soup

This soup betrays its Portuguese origins in the use of poached eggs in a soup.

*Ingredients* (6 servings)  Preparation time: 20 minutes
Cooking time: 20 minutes

1 cup finely chopped coriander leaf (cilantro)
6 eggs poached
3 slices of bread deep-fried golden brown
2 tablespoons vegetable oil
6 cups chicken stock
Salt to taste
Black pepper to taste

*Preparation*
1. Finely chop coriander.
2. Poach the eggs.

3. Deep-fry the bread, dry on paper towels, and slice in quarters.
4. Heat the chicken stock and the coriander for about 10 minutes.
5. Add salt and pepper.
6. To serve: Place 1 cup soup in bowl; add 2 quarters of slice of toast, top with poached egg.

## Coriander Leaf (Cilantro) and Green Pea Soup

*Ingredients* (4 Servings)　　　　　　　　　　　　　　Preparation time: 20 minutes
　　　　　　　　　　　　　　　　　　　　　　　　　Cooking time: 15 minutes

1 ½ tablespoons butter
⅓ cup all-purpose flour
4 cups warm beef stock
¼ cup milk
2 tablespoons fresh coriander leaf (cilantro), finely chopped
Salt to taste
4 tablespoons cooked green peas

*Preparation*
1. In a saucepan heat the butter over a low flame. When it bubbles, throw in the flour, and stir until it turns pale brown.
2. Gradually add the warm beef stock, a little at a time, stirring continually to avoid lumps. Bring the mixture to a boil.
3. Immediately lower the heat, add milk and fresh coriander leaf (cilantro), and simmer for 10 minutes, stirring occasionally.
4. Taste and add salt as desired.
5. Place a tablespoon of cooked peas in bowl and top with a ladleful of the soup. Serve hot.

## Cucumber Soup I

Cucumber soups are refreshing when served cold in the summertime.

*Ingredients* (4 servings)　　　　　　　　　　　　　　Preparation time: 20 minutes
　　　　　　　　　　　　　　　　　　　　　　　　　Cooking time: 15 minutes

¼ cup butter
2 tablespoons flour
4 cups warm chicken stock
2 medium size cucumbers (about 8 inches long)
1 cup thick cream (ideally whipping cream, but half-and-half may be substituted)

1. In a saucepan melt butter over low heat until it bubbles. Add the flour and mix into a smooth paste. Remove pan from heat.
2. Add the chicken stock, a little at a time, stirring continually, until it is smooth and free of lumps.

3. Peel and de-seed cucumbers. In a blender, puree one cucumber. Dice the other cucumber into ¼ inch pieces and set aside.
4. Add the pureed cucumber to the broth, sir and then add the chopped cucumber.
5. Simmer the broth over a low heat for 10 minutes.
6. Add the cream and gently blend and heat through.
7. Serve hot or chilled.

**Cucumber Soup II**

*Ingredients* (4 servings)                                   Preparation time: 25 minutes
                                                             Cooking time: 20 minutes

1 ½ tablespoons vegetable or olive oil
1 large onion (finely chopped)
2 cucumbers (about 28 ozs), peeled, de-seeded and cut into coarse chunks
4 cups chicken stock
2 tablespoons butter
¼ cup flour
A few sprigs of mint
⅓ cup milk
Salt to taste

*Preparation*
1. In a medium-size saucepan, heat the oil and sauté in it the onion till it turns, translucent. Do NOT let it brown.
2. Add the cucumber and chicken stock, and allow to cook for 15 minutes.
3. In a separate small pan melt the butter, stir in the flour. Allow to cook for 1 minute (this makes a roux).
4. In the blender, pour the soup mixture, the roux and the mint leaves. Blend until the mixture is smooth and homogeneous.
5. Return to the large pan; add the milk and the salt. Simmer for 10 minutes.
6. Serve either hot or chilled.

**Vegetable Soup**

*Ingredients* (4 servings)                                   Preparation time: 20 minutes
                                                             Cooking time: 45 minutes

3 medium carrots
4 medium turnips
6 cups of water
Salt to taste
Pepper to taste
Croutons to garnish

*Preparation*
1. Grate carrots and turnips using a fine vegetable grater.
2. Heat water, and add carrots, turnips, salt and pepper.
3. Serve piping hot with croutons.

## Asparagus Soup

Since asparagus is not a local Goan vegetable, the canned variety is used in this recipe.

*Ingredients* (4 servings)  　　　　　　　　　　　Preparation time: 20 minutes
　　　　　　　　　　　　　　　　　　　　　　　　Cooking time: 20 minutes

½ cup butter
2 tablespoons flour
4 cups chicken stock
6-8 white asparagus spears
2 cups whipping cream
4 green asparagus tips

*Preparation*
1. Melt butter and stir in the flour.
2. Add chicken stock and stir thoroughly.
3. Blend white asparagus and add to stock.
4. Add whipping cream.
5. Garnish with green asparagus tips.
6. Serve hot.

## *Dal* (Lentil) Soup

*Ingredients* (4 servings)  　　　　　　　　　　　Preparation time: 15 minutes
　　　　　　　　　　　　　　　　　　　　　　　　Cooking time: 25 minutes

1 cup *masoor dal* (orange colored lentils)
1 medium onion finely chopped
3 tablespoons butter
1 tomato, peeled and finely chopped
4-½ to 5 cups chicken broth
1 tablespoon flour
½ cup milk
Croutons to garnish

*Preparation*
1. Wash the *dal* until the water is clear. Drain thoroughly and set aside.
2. Sauté the chopped onion in butter until lightly gold, but not brown.
3. Add the tomato and cook until soft.

4. Add the *dal* to the onion-tomato mixture, and then add the chicken broth.
5. Cook until the lentils are soft.
6. Cool and puree in a blender.
7. Serve chilled: garnish with homemade croutons.
8. To serve hot: add, at serving time, an enrichment made by melting 1 tablespoon of butter and adding to it 1 tablespoon flour and ½ cup of milk, which is brought to a boil. Gradually incorporate this into the soup which is warmed, making sure to dissolve all lumps. This thickens the soup.

## *Sopa de Camarão*
### (Prawn Soup)

*Ingredients* (4 servings)

Preparation time: 20 minutes
Cooking time: 20 minutes

½ lb of fresh, medium size prawns
6 spring onions finely chopped
1 teaspoon finely chopped fresh ginger
¼ cup of coconut milk (see "Useful Tips" section)
8 cups of water
Salt to taste
Pepper to taste
1 cup of croutons

*Preparation*
1. Peel and devein prawns.
2. Finely chop spring onions and ginger.
3. Prepare ¼ cup of coconut milk (see "Useful Tips" section).
4. Boil prawns in 8 cups of water.
5. Add spring onions, ginger, coconut milk, salt and pepper and stir well.
6. Serve piping hot; add croutons to garnish.

## Bacon Soup

*Ingredients* (4 servings)

Preparation time: 20 minutes
Cooking time: 20 minutes

4 strips bacon
¼ cup flour
4 cups warm beef stock
3 oz vermicelli or thin spaghetti
Salt to taste

*Preparation*
1. Fry the bacon strips in a deep skillet until the bacon is crisp. Drain on absorbent paper, crumble the bacon, and set it aside.
2. To the bacon fat, add the flour and stir until the mixture is a golden brown.
3. Gradually add the warm stock, stirring continually to dissolve any lumps.
4. Bring to a boil and add the vermicelli which has been cut into 1 inch pieces.
5. Lower the flame and simmer for 15 minutes. Add salt if needed.
6. Serve the soup in individual bowls garnished with crumbled bacon.

# Appetizers

Like soups, these are a Western import into Goan cuisine. In fact, they are seldom used as "starters' to a meal, serving rather as snacks to be offered to guests or visitors who may drop in, or as part of a high tea in the late afternoon.

## *Rissoes de Camarão*
(Prawn Puffs)

*Ingredients*

Preparation time: 45 minutes
Cooking time: 30 minutes

*For the filling*
½ lb medium-size prawns
1 cup milk
2 tablespoons grated cheese
1 tablespoon butter
1 ½ tablespoons flour
3 green (jalapeno or serrano) chilies, remove seeds

*For the pastry*
½ cup water
1 tablespoon butter
1 teaspoon salt
1 teaspoon baking powder
1½ cups sifted flour
2 eggs
½ cup bread crumbs

*Preparation*
1. Peel, devein and chop the prawns.
2. *For the filling*, prepare a thick white sauce with the milk, cheese, butter, flour, and chilies, to which is added the chopped prawns.
3. *For the pastry*, boil the water with butter and salt. Add the baking powder and flour to the boiling mixture and stir well. Cool the mixture, place on a rolling sheet, and knead till smooth. Roll out fine and cut in rounds.
4. Place filling in the rounds, fold over and pinch the edges closed with water.
5. Roll the rounds in two beaten eggs and bread crumbs.
6. Deep-fry the stuffed rounds (*rissoes*).

## *Fofos de Peixe*
(Fish Rolls)

*Ingredients*

Preparation time: 45 minutes
Cooking time: 30 minutes

¾ lb fleshy fish
½ cup water
1 teaspoon salt
3 medium potatoes
2 eggs
1 tablespoon butter
2 tablespoons grated cheese
½ teaspoon chili powder
2 whole eggs
2 tablespoons cold water
1 cup fine breadcrumbs
Salt to taste

*Preparation*
1. Boil the fish in ½ cup of water with 1 teaspoon of salt until cooked.
2. Boil and mash the potatoes.
3. Shred the fish and add to the potatoes and blend well.
4. Add the eggs, butter, cheese, and chili powder and blend well.
5. Shape into cylindrical rolls, about an inch in diameter and about 3 inches long.
6. Beat the other two eggs with the cold water in a shallow container.
7. Dip the roll in breadcrumbs, then dip in the egg mixture and again in bread crumbs until there is a thick even coat. Refrigerate for about an hour.
8. Bake in an oven pre-heated to 350°F for 15-20 minutes, turning once, until they are a nice golden brown. Or you may deep-fry in hot oil.

*Note:* These fish rolls were often made with '*bacalhau*', dried and salted cod, which was imported into Goa from Portugal. The *bacalhau* has to be soaked overnight in cold water to soften and desalinate it. Discard the water and then use instead of the fish. *Bacalhau* is available in some ethnic food markets.

To serve as a first course, the fish rolls were accompanied by a white sauce.

To make the sauce: melt over low heat 1 tablespoon of butter, stir in 1 tablespoon of flour, 2 tablespoons of grated cheese and 1 cup of milk. Stir until sauce thickens. If a thinner sauce is desired, increase the quantity of milk.

## *Empadinhas*
(Small Pork Pies)

*Ingredients* (18 empadinhas)

Preparation time: 45 minutes
Cooking time: 20 minutes

*For the filling*
2 green (jalapeno or serrano) chilies
1 red chili
1 clove garlic
1 tablespoon ginger
½ teaspoon cumin seeds
½ teaspoon turmeric
6 peppercorns
1 tablespoon cinnamon
6 cloves
½ tablespoon white vinegar
1 lb pork finely cut
6 medium onions finely cut
2 tablespoons vegetable oil
Salt to taste

*For the pastry*
½ lb flour
½ teaspoon baking powder
3 egg yolks
1 tablespoon vegetable oil
½ cup powdered sugar
¼ teaspoon salt
Beaten egg yolk for brushing *empadinha* tops

*Preparation*
1. Grind the spices listed under filling with the vinegar to form a paste (*masala*).
2. Add the diced pork and mix well.
3. Lightly brown the onions in vegetable oil.
4. Add the pork mixture to the onions and cook well, adding a small amount of water and salt to taste.
5. Set aside when the mixture is well cooked and relatively dry.
6. Knead the pastry elements together and roll them out into thin dough (do not add water).
7. Lightly grease 18 small round pastry molds.
8. Line pastry molds with the dough, allowing sufficient overflow to top the mold when filled.
9. Fill each mold with the pork mixture.
10. Fold over the dough to cover the top of the filling completely.
11. Brush the tops of the *empadinhas* with egg yolk.
12. Place in an oven preheated to 350°F and bake until golden brown.
13. Serve warm.

## *Fofos de Queijo*
(Cheese Puffs)

*Ingredients*

Preparation time: 15 minutes
Cooking time: 10 minutes

4 eggs
1 small onion finely chopped
½ cup flour
½ teaspoon salt
1 teaspoon baking powder
⅓ lb grated cheese
Vegetable oil for deep frying

*Preparation*
1. Beat together the yolks and whites of the eggs.
2. Add the chopped onion, flour, salt, baking powder and grated cheese and mix thoroughly.
3. Bring oil to a boil, and drop in teaspoonfuls of the mixture.
4. Fry to a golden brown.
5. Dry on paper towels
6. Serve warm.

## Shrimp Toast

*Ingredients*

Preparation time: 40 minutes
Cooking time: 30 minutes

4 oz shrimp--shelled and deveined
⅛ teaspoon salt
⅛ teaspoon black pepper
1 tablespoon olive oil
1 lemon slice, coarsely chopped
2 tablespoons grated Parmesan cheese
1 small green (jalapeno or serrano) chili, de-seeded, very finely chopped
¼ teaspoon lemon juice
5 slices of day-old sandwich bread
Vegetable oil for frying bread slices
Green pepper and tomato strips for garnish

*Preparation*
1. Season the shrimp with salt and pepper and allow to stand for 15 minutes.
2. In a small saucepan, put in the olive oil, the chopped slice of lemon, the shrimp and the cheese and cook on a low flame till the mixture is almost dry.
3. Cool and process the mixture through a blender or food processor, until it forms a paste.
4. Add the finely chopped green chili and the lemon juice, and blend thoroughly with a fork.
5. Trim the bread slice, cut into triangles. Deep fry in hot oil and drain on absorbent paper towels.
6. Apply the prepared shrimp paste to the fried bread slices.
7. Decorate with the green pepper and tomato strips.

## *Forminhas*
### (Tartlets)

These are dainty miniature fluted pastry molds served with a variety of fillings. The molds are available at gourmet kitchen stores in a variety of shapes - round, triangular and boat-shaped. The cases can be baked and kept in an airtight container for two or three weeks. They are then filled with a filling at serving time. Preparation time for the filling varies according to ingredients used.

Preparation time: 30 minutes plus refrigeration time
Baking time for each batch: 7 – 10 minutes

*Ingredients*

*Pastry crust*
1 cup all-purpose flour
½ teaspoon of salt
⅓ cup cold butter, cut into small cubes
⅔ tablespoon of chilled water

*Preparation*
1. Add salt to the flour, and working only with the fingertips, rub the butter cubes into the flour, till the mixture resembles breadcrumbs. Add enough chilled water just to bind the dough. Refrigerate the dough for at least half an hour.
2. Spread the dough onto to a cold surface until it is about an eighth of an inch thick.
3. Mold into the pastry cases, and prick the surface lightly with a fork.
4. Bake in a 275°F oven for about 7-10 minutes. Since oven temperatures vary, make sure the oven is not too hot. As the proportion of butter is very high, it will burn and produce an acrid taste if the oven is too hot. Dough should suffice for 2 to 2½ dozen pastry cases.

*Fillings*: Individual taste and creativity in relation to available ingredients is all that determines the type of savory fillings for these hors-d'oeuvres. Listed below are some suggestions.

(1) Small cubes of cooked chicken combined with cooked corn, bound together with a cheese sauce. (You may use the recipe for the sauce for fish rolls, flavoring the sauce with a cheese of your choice).
(2) Small bay shrimp in a white sauce, spiked with green chili to taste.
(3) Assorted vegetables—cooked peas, cubed carrots, cubed beets, and thinly sliced green beans flavored with mayonnaise.
(4) Shredded cabbage and green and red bell peppers moistened with French dressing and a little mustard paste.

## Meat patties

*Ingredients*

Preparation time: 50 minutes
Cooking time: 45 minutes

*Pastry*
1 cup all-purpose flour
½ teaspoon salt

2 tablespoons vegetable shortening
Enough chilled water (1 – 2 tablespoons) to bind the dough

*Preparation*
1. Mix together the flour and salt. Cut in the shortening until the mixture is crumbly. Add enough water to make a malleable dough. Allow it to rest for at least ½ an hour.
2. Roll out the dough onto a lightly floured board, into a rectangle (approx.15"W x 18"L), and about ⅛ inch thick. Cut lengthwise into strips about 3 inches wide and 4½ inches long. The stuffed patty looks like a mini-pillow.

*Filling*
1 lb lean ground beef
1 teaspoon salt
½ teaspoon turmeric powder
3 red Kashmiri chilies *or* ½ teaspoon Kashmiri chili powder
4 peppercorns *or* ¼ teaspoon black pepper
2 garlic cloves
1 piece about ½ inch long of fresh ginger
½ teaspoon cumin seeds
½ teaspoon coriander seeds
4 cloves
¼ teaspoon cinnamon
2- 3 tablespoons white vinegar (as required, to grind the seasonings to a paste)
2 tablespoons cooking oil
1 small onion, finely chopped
1 small tomato, finely chopped
1 green (jalapeno or serrano) chili, finely chopped
Small bunch of coriander leaves (cilantro), finely chopped
1 teaspoon sugar

*Preparation*
1. Season the meat with the salt and turmeric and set aside.
2. Grind all the spices with the vinegar until you get a smooth paste and set aside.
3. In a suitably-sized saucepan heat the oil, and sauté the onion until it is soft but NOT brown.
4. Add the ground paste and cook for about 2 minutes. Add the tomato and the green chilies and cook until they soften.
5. Add the seasoned meat and ½ cup water. Cover the saucepan and allow the meat to cook on a low flame for about 20 minutes, or until most of the water is evaporated. The mixture has to be on the dry side.
6. Add the sugar and chopped coriander leaves (cilantro).
7. In the center of each pastry strip, place one rounded teaspoonful of the filling. Double the strip so that all sides touch, seal with plain water. With the edge of the fork tines, press down all the sides so that they are completely sealed.
8. Deep fry the patties in hot oil, and drain on paper towels before serving.

## B. Fish and Seafood

*Peixe Recheado* (Mackerels stuffed with spices)
*Ambot Tik* (Sour and Hot Fish)
Goa Fish Curry
Prawn Cutlets
*Peixe Vermelho* (Red Fish)
*Pará de Peixe* (Sour Fish)
*Thisrio* (Clams)
*Sunkattam Koddi* (Prawn Curry) – *pictured on page 53*
*Apa de Camarão* (Prawn Pie)
*Poios* (Small Shrimp Patties)
*Empada de Ostras (*Oyster Pie)
*Bombil Fish* (Fried Fresh *Bombay Duck*) – *pictured on page 53*
*Sukhe Bombil* (Dried *Bombay Duck*)
Sautéed Prawns – *pictured on page 54*
Squid
Salmon Aspic
Salmon Cutlets

## B. Fish and Seafood

Fish and seafood are the principal sources of protein in the Goan diet of the common man, and they are regular features of daily meals. Fish and seafood are caught in the sea that breaks on the long Goan coastline and in the inland rivers. Fishermen return with their catch by 4 or 5 pm, which is then covered with ice and delivered to the market between 6 and 8 pm by fisherwomen in wicker baskets, and sold immediately.

Some of the fish and seafood will be readily recognizable to Western readers of this book -- prawns, mussels, baby shark, salmon, mackerel, and oysters. Others like "*Bombay duck*" are local favorites and there are no Western equivalents. Also, the taste of tropical fish is different-- for example, as in the case of mackerel -- from the same fish caught in colder waters.

Fish and seafood are generally served with rice, and, perhaps, a central form of curry. For example, a prawn curry with rice could be accompanied by a stuffed fish (*peixe recheado*) or by sour and hot fish (*ambot tik.*)

On festive occasions, a whole steamed fish cooked with spices, or accompanied by mayonnaise, appears as part of a more elaborate menu.

### *Peixe Recheado*
(Mackerels stuffed with spices)

Although this dish is traditionally made with mackerel, those who prefer a non-oily fish, can use pomfret or pompano.

*Ingredients*                                                             Preparation time: 25 minutes
                                                                          Cooking time: 15 minutes

6 mackerels (pomfret or pompano can also be used)
1 teaspoon salt
12 dry red Kashmiri chilies
8 peppercorns
1 tablespoon chopped garlic
¼ teaspoon ground cumin seed
2 teaspoons coriander powder
½ teaspoon turmeric
¼ to ⅓ cup white vinegar (for grinding spices)
1 teaspoon tamarind juice (see "Useful Tips" section)
½ cup oil for frying

*Preparation*
1. Clean the mackerel, removing fins and entrails and wash well.
2. Slice each mackerel lengthwise along both sides of the spine. If desired remove spine.
3. Lightly salt each fish and set aside.
4. Prepare a *masala* or *mirem* by grinding the spices listed above in vinegar to form a paste.

5. Stuff the *masala* or *mirem* in each mackerel on both sides of the main spine.
6. Fry each stuffed mackerel in hot oil until well cooked.
7. Dry on paper towels and serve hot.


## *Ambot Tik*
(Sour and Hot Fish)

*Ingredients*  Preparation time: 25 minutes
Cooking time: 20-30 minutes

1 lb baby shark (or skate, or catfish)
1 medium onion, finely chopped
1 tablespoon vegetable oil
1 tablespoon tamarind juice (See "Useful Tips" section)
1 tablespoon chili powder
¼ teaspoon turmeric
½ teaspoon coriander powder
¼ teaspoon finely chopped fresh ginger
½ teaspoon black pepper
¼ teaspoon cumin powder
½ teaspoon finely chopped fresh ginger
1 tablespoon white vinegar
(In Goa, the peel(s) of *solans de brindão*, a typical dried sour fruit, are added. Unfortunately, these are not readily available outside Goa)

*Preparation*
1. Cut the fish horizontally into small size pieces.
2. Fry the onion until lightly brown in vegetable oil.
3. Add tamarind juice, vinegar and spices to 1½ cups of warm water and mix thoroughly.
4. Add this mixture to the onions and bring to a boil and let simmer for 10-15 minutes.
5. Add the fish to the mixture, add more water if necessary, and cook for 10-15 minutes, or until done.


## Goa Fish Curry

*Ingredients*  Preparation time: 25-30 minutes
Cooking time: 35 minutes

1 *pomfret* or similar fish (*e.g.*, white pompano, mahi mahi)
Salt to taste
Juice of 1 lemon
2 tablespoons oil
1 medium onion, coarsely chopped
¼ teaspoon cumin powder

¼ teaspoon chopped fresh garlic
½ teaspoon tamarind juice (see "Useful tips" section)
4 green (jalapeno or serrano) chilies, chopped coarsely
1 teaspoon fresh ginger, coarsely chopped
½ teaspoon turmeric
6 dry Kashmiri chilies
Water to moisten paste
1 cup coconut milk (see "Useful Tips" section)

*Preparation*
1. Clean the pomfret, wash and slice horizontally into pieces.
2. Sprinkle the pomfret with salt and lemon juice and chill in refrigerator for 30 minutes.
3. Sautee the chopped onion with 1 – 2 tablespoons of oil.
4. Grind the spices with the tamarind juice and chopped green chilies with enough water to make a paste. (The water should be barely sufficient to moisten it).
5. Add the coconut milk
6. Cook the mixture and bring it to a boil.
7. Lower the heat and simmer the mixture for 10-15 minutes.
8. Add the fish and cook until done (about 10-15 minutes).
9. Serve with boiled or steamed rice.

**Prawn Cutlets**

*Ingredients*                                     Preparation time: 45 minutes
                                                  Cooking time: 15 minutes

½ lb large prawns
1 small onion sliced fine
3 small green (jalapeno or serrano) chilies, chopped fine
6 cloves garlic
½ teaspoon turmeric
½ teaspoon black pepper
1 teaspoon salt
2 tablespoons white vinegar
4 tablespoons vegetable oil
1 egg beaten lightly
Bread crumbs
Lettuce leaves to garnish

*Preparation*
1. Shell and devein the prawns, retaining the tails.
2. Cut down the center of each prawn and open it out flat.
3. Grind the spices lightly together in the vinegar and add salt and pepper.
4. Marinate the prawns with the mixture of spices, store in the refrigerator for 30 minutes.
5. Heat the vegetable oil in a frying pan.
6. Roll each prawn in the egg mixture and bread crumbs, fry to golden brown on both sides.
7. Serve on a bed of lettuce.

## *Peixe Vermelho*
(Red Fish)

*Ingredients*                                         Preparation time: 35 minutes
                                                      Cooking time: 25 minutes

½ lb fish (such as pomfret, pompano, mahi mahi)
1½ cups water
1 sliced large onion
8 peppercorns
Salt to taste

*Sauce*
1 tablespoon chopped ginger
12 cloves of garlic
1 medium onion, finely chopped
2 tablespoons vegetable oil
4 medium tomatoes, cut in quarters

*Preparation*
1. Cook the fish for about 15 minutes in 1½ cups of water with the sliced onion, peppercorns and salt.
2. Set aside the fish stock.
3. Grind together the garlic and ginger.
4. Fry the onion until golden brown in the vegetable oil, add the garlic and ginger, and the tomatoes and cook for about 5 minutes.
5. Add the fish stock and cook until it thickens. If necessary, add a small amount of flour.
6. Cool the sauce for 5 minutes.
7. Arrange the fish as desired on a serving plate. Pour the sauce over the fish. Serve hot.


## *Pará de Peixe*
(Sour Fish)

*Ingredients*                                         Preparation time: 40 minutes
                                                      Cooking time: 10 minutes

½ lb long red Kashmiri chilies
½ lb whole cloves (mashed)
1 tablespoon ground cumin seeds
½ tablespoon red pepper
½ teaspoon turmeric
½ cup white vinegar
3 lb of salted medium-size (mackerel) fish
Vegetable oil for frying fish

*Preparation*
1. Grind the spices together with a little bit of vinegar to form a *masala/mirem*.
2. In a wide-mouth jar, place one fish with a layer of *masala/mirem*, followed by another fish and *masala/mirem*, until all the fish and *masala/mirem* have been used.
3. Fill the jar with vinegar so that the fish are completely covered.
4. Seal the jar tightly, and store it in a cool place for 7-10 days to properly marinate fish.
5. To serve, remove one or more fish, as required, fry in vegetable oil, and serve.

### *Thisrio*
(Clams)

*Ingredients*

Preparation time: 40 minutes
Cooking time: 20 minutes

24 small clams (Manila mussels, available in Chinese groceries, can also be used for this dish)
1 inch fresh ginger, peeled and coarsely chopped
8 cloves of garlic, peeled
1 ½ cups of water
4 tablespoons vegetable oil
2 medium onions, chopped fine
1-2 green (jalapeno or serrano) chilies, sliced into rounds
½ teaspoon turmeric powder
2 teaspoon cumin powder
½ tomato, cut into small cubes
½ fresh coconut, finely grated (see "Useful Tips" section)
½ teaspoon salt
3 or 4 *solans de brindão* (not readily available outside Goa) (optional)

*Preparation*
1. Wash and scrub the clams.
2. Blend to a smooth paste the ginger and garlic with ½ cup of water.
3. Heat oil in a large pot over medium heat. Sauté onions until translucent.
4. Add ginger and garlic paste, green chilies, turmeric, and cumin. Fry and stir for a minute.
5. Add the chopped tomato and cook for 2 minutes.
6. Add coconut, salt, and one cup of water. Bring to a boil.
7. Add clams, mix well and bring to a boil.
8. Cover tightly. Lower heat slightly and let clams steam for 5-10 minutes until they open.
9. Serve hot.

### *Sunkattam Koddi* – *pictured on page 53*
### (Prawn Curry)

*Ingredients*

Preparation time: 20 minutes
Cooking time: 10 minutes

2 tablespoons vegetable oil
1 medium onion, finely chopped
½ teaspoon cumin powder
2 teaspoons coriander powder
½ teaspoon turmeric
½ teaspoon red chili powder
4 garlic cloves, finely chopped
1 small green (jalapeno or serrano) chili, finely chopped
2 teaspoons tamarind juice (see "Useful Tips" section)
1 cup coconut milk (see "Useful Tips" section)
1 lb fresh prawns, cleaned and deveined

*Preparation*
1. Heat oil and fry onion until golden.
2. Add cumin, coriander, turmeric, red chili powder, garlic, green chili, and tamarind juice. Mix.
3. Add coconut milk, and mix thoroughly.
4. Add prawns and small amount of water; cook until prawns are pink (about 10 minutes).
5. Serve with steamed rice, pickles and chutneys.

### *Apa de Camarão*
### (Prawn Pie)

*Ingredients*

Preparation time: 60 minutes
Cooking time: 30-45 minutes

*For Pie*
1 medium tender coconut, grated fine (see "Useful Tips" section)
¾ cup water
6 slices of white bread (5 oz)
6 eggs
1 tablespoon butter
¼ teaspoon of salt
2 teaspoons sugar
Butter for greasing baking dish
Egg yolk for glazing pie

*Shrimp Filling*
1 onion, finely diced
1 small piece of ginger (about ½ inch in length)
6 cloves garlic, finely chopped
2 tablespoons vegetable oil
6 green (jalapeno or serrano) chilies, finely chopped
1 teaspoon red chili powder

¼ teaspoon of black pepper
1 teaspoon saffron or turmeric
1 teaspoon sugar
1 lb fresh prawns, shelled, deveined, and salted

*Preparation*

*For Pie*
1. Add water to the coconut, and then add shredded bread. Set aside for one hour.
2. Add egg yolks, butter, salt, and sugar. Mix well by hand. If the paste is thick, add water.
3. Beat the egg whites and fold into the above mixed batter.

*For Shrimp Filling*
1. Fry the onion, ginger and garlic in oil, until golden.
2. Add all the spices and mix well while frying.
3. Add the prawns and cook until soft.

*Assembling of Prawn Pie*
1. In a greased baking dish (10 inches square, 2 inch high) spread half of the batter and bake for 5 minutes in a 300°F oven.
2. Add the prawn filling.
3. Top with the remainder of the batter.
4. Cook at 300°F for approximately ½ hour. Check for readiness by using a toothpick. If the pie is ready, the toothpick should come out clean/dry.
5. Glaze top of pie with egg yolk, and cook for 5 minutes.
6. Cut into slices and serve hot or cold.

## *Poios*
### (Small Prawn Patties)

*Ingredients*     Preparation time: 20 minutes
                  Cooking time: 10 minutes

1 cup of medium prawns, peeled, cleaned and deveined
4 cloves of garlic
1 teaspoon of *mirem/ masala/*ground paste (see "Useful Tips" section)
8 to 10 cumin seeds
Enough white vinegar to grind the above ingredients into a malleable paste

*Preparation*
1. Grind the above ingredients into a paste (it should be moist and able to hold a shape.)
2. Shape into rounds the size of a quarter and about ¾ inch thick.
3. Fry in a little oil, until they are a light brown color on both sides.

## *Empada de Ostras*
(Oyster Pie)

*Ingredients*

Preparation time: 30 minutes
Cooking time: 25 minutes

*Filling*
Grind to a paste:
   10 garlic cloves
   ¾ inch piece of ginger, sliced
   ¼ teaspoon of ground cinnamon
   5 whole cloves
   ¼ teaspoon turmeric
   ¼ teaspoon nutmeg
   ½ cup white vinegar

36 medium size oysters in their own juice
2 tablespoons oil (olive oil is the best)
3 medium size onions, chopped fine
1 large tomato, peeled, deseeded, and chopped fine
2 hardboiled eggs, sliced in rounds
2 boiled white potatoes, peeled and cubed into ½ inch cubes

*For the pie topping*
3 egg yolks
2 ½ tablespoons sugar
¼ lb flour
¼ lb semolina
½ teaspoon salt
1 oz butter

*Preparation*
1. Grind all the spices to a paste with the vinegar.
2. Drain the oysters, save the juice and set aside.
3. In a saucepan heat the oil, and sauté the onions until they are soft, but not brown.
4. Add the spice mixture and fry for 2 minutes.
5. Add the tomato and cook for 2 minutes until soft.
6. Add the oysters, with about ⅓ to ½ cup of the oyster juice and cook until the oysters are done. Five minutes is usually sufficient. There should be some gravy in this filling but it should not overwhelm the oysters.
7. Let the mixture cool.

*For the pie topping*
1. Beat the egg yolks with the sugar and set aside.
2. Mix the flour, semolina, salt and butter, with your finger tips until the butter is incorporated into the mixture.
3. Add the yolk/sugar mixture. Keep on working the mixture until it is granular, not smooth.

*Assembling the pie*
1. In a pyrex dish, place half of the filling.
2. Layer the cubed potatoes and sliced eggs over the filling.
3. Place another layer of the filling and top with the granulated topping.
4. Preheat the oven to 375°F. Place pie in the oven and watch carefully. The topping should be a golden brown. Usual baking time is 10-15 minutes.

### *Bombil* **Fish** – *pictured on page 53*
### (Fried Fresh *Bombay Duck*)

*Note:* There is no equivalent for this fish in the West.

*Ingredients*                                                     Preparation time: 20 minutes
                                                                  Cooking time: 15 minutes

6 medium or large *Bombay Duck* (*bombil* fish)
¾ cup flour
½ teaspoon turmeric
½ teaspoon chili powder
Salt to taste
2 eggs beaten
Vegetable oil for frying

*Preparation*
1. Slice each cleaned fish lengthwise and remove the center bone.
2. Place each fish in a flat open position between two paper towels and place pressure on top to maintain it open.
3. Mix flour, turmeric, chili powder, and salt.
4. Dip each fish in egg lightly and then in the above mixture.
5. Fry until golden brown.
6. Lay on clean paper towel to drain excess oil. Serve hot.

### **Sukhe Bombil**
### (Dried *Bombay Duck*)

*Ingredients*                                                     Preparation time: 25 minutes
                                                                  Cooking time: 20 minutes

6 dried *Bombay Ducks* (*bombil* fish)
1 large onion, finely chopped
2 tablespoons vegetable oil
3 green (jalapeno or serrano) chilies, finely chopped
1 teaspoon tamarind juice (see "Useful Tips" section)
Salt to taste

*Preparation*
1. Cut each *Bombay Duck* (*bombil*) in half horizontally and soak in water.
2. Sauté onion in oil until golden. Add tamarind juice and chilies and stir while cooking for 5 minutes.
3. Add *Bombay Ducks* (*bombil*) and salt and cook until done (5-10 minutes).
4. Drain on paper towels. Serve hot.

**Sautéed Prawns** – *pictured on page 54*

*Ingredients*

Preparation time: 35 minutes
Cooking time: 10 minutes

2 tablespoons vegetable oil
1 medium onion, cut in rings
¼ teaspoon turmeric
1 green (jalapeno or serrano) chili, finely chopped
3 garlic cloves, finely chopped
½ teaspoon ginger, finely chopped
½ lb small to medium size prawns, shelled and deveined
Salt to taste

*Preparation*
1. Fry the onion in oil until golden.
2. Add the spices and stir thoroughly.
3. Add the prawns and cook until pink (about 5 minutes).
4. Serve hot with white rice or spaghetti.

**Squid**

*Ingredients*

Preparation time: 30 minutes
Cooking time: 30 minutes

1 dozen squid
1 large onion, cut fine
1 tablespoon vegetable oil
1 clove of garlic, cut fine
1 peeled tomato, cut fine
1 level teaspoon red chili powder
1 tablespoon white vinegar
1 teaspoon salt

*For the gravy*
1 medium size onion cut fine
1 medium size tomato cut fine
Oil for frying
Water

*Preparation*
1. Clean and wash the squid thoroughly. Separate the head and tentacles from the body.
2. Mince the squid heads and tentacles.
3. Fry the onion in oil, adding the sliced garlic and tomato.
4. Add the minced squid and fry lightly.
5. Add the chili powder, vinegar, and ½ teaspoon of salt, and fry until the minced squid is about half cooked.
6. Salt the squid bodies with the remaining salt and insert the minced squid mixture. Join the ends of the squid with a toothpick.
7. Make a gravy with a medium onion cut fine, and a medium tomato cut fine. Fry lightly in oil. Add the squid and a small amount of water and cook until the squid is done.
8. Serve hot with rice.

**Salmon Aspic**

Aspics were served mostly at weddings or as a buffet offering at large significant family gatherings.

*Ingredients*                              Preparation time: 45 minutes
                                           Cooking time: 15 minutes

*For the mayonnaise*
3 hard-boiled eggs
1 teaspoon white vinegar
⅓ - ½ cup milk
Salt and sugar to taste

*For the aspic*
1- 12 oz can tomato juice
Juice of 1 lemon
Pinch of sugar (⅛ teaspoon)
Pinch of ground mustard (⅛ teaspoon)
2 teaspoons of Knox gelatin
¾ lb salmon, skinless and boneless (fresh is best, but a high-quality well-drained canned salmon is also acceptable)
1 teaspoon black pepper
Lettuce leaves, olives, and red bell peppers to garnish

*Preparation*
1. Separate the yolks and the whites from the hardboiled eggs. Mash the egg yolks with the vinegar. Add the milk, a little at a time, until you get a creamy consistency to make a mayonnaise. Season with salt and sugar. Slice the egg whites into fine strips.
2. Heat the tomato juice and bring to a boil over medium heat. Add half the lemon juice, the sugar and the mustard and stir to blend thoroughly.

3. In a small bowl, soak the gelatin in 3 tablespoons of cold water until softened. Dissolve the gelatin thoroughly in the hot tomato juice.
4. In a wet mold, pour the tomato juice to a height of about ½ inch. Refrigerate immediately. To the rest of the tomato juice, add the salmon, pepper, the rest of the lemon juice, the prepared mayonnaise and the strips of egg white.
5. Wait till the tomato juice in the wet mold is completely set, then pack this mixture tightly into the mold. Refrigerate for several hours.
6. To unmold: Dip the mold in very hot water for about 30 seconds or a while longer if necessary. Turn it upside down on a platter--a glass dish is best.
7. Decorate with lettuce leaves, olives, red bell peppers and radishes carved into flower shapes.

## Salmon Cutlets

This is usually served at lunch with either a white sauce or a tomato sauce, accompanied by a salad of fresh greens.

*Ingredients*   Preparation time: 30 minutes
Cooking time: 20 minutes

1-15 oz can of red salmon (crabmeat or shrimp may also be used)
1 egg, lightly beaten
2 tablespoons butter
1 medium onion, finely chopped
1 green bell pepper, finely chopped
1 clove of garlic, minced
1 or 2 green (jalapeno or serrano) chilies, finely chopped (to diminish the piquancy, de-seed the chilies)
1 teaspoon or less of salt
½ teaspoon black pepper

*For the coating*
½ cup fine breadcrumbs
1 egg lightly beaten

*For frying*: 1 cup of oil

*Preparation*
1. Drain the salmon and then flake it into a bowl. Add the egg, mix well and set aside.
2. Melt the butter over low heat, add the onion, bell pepper, garlic, chilies and cook until soft. Combine this mixture with the salmon/egg mixture, season with salt and pepper and mix thoroughly. Refrigerate, covered, for a couple of hours until the mixture is firm.
3. To make the cutlets, shape into ovals about 4-5 inches long and about 2½ inches wide (about half a cup per cutlet). Dip the cutlet into the crumbs, then the egg and then the crumbs again. Refrigerate for another half hour, so that the coating adheres to the cutlet.

4. In a skillet, heat the oil over medium heat, and fry the cutlets a few at a time, until golden brown (about 4 to 5 minutes on each side).
5. Drain on paper towels and serve as soon as possible.

*Sunkattam Koddi (Prawn Curry)*

*Fried Fresh Bombay Duck (Bombil Fish)*

*Sautéed Prawns*

*Fried Pomfret (Pompano)*

## C. Meats and Poultry

*Xacuti* – pictured on page 67

Chicken Curry – *pictured on page 67*

*Sarapatel* – *pictured on page 68*

*Cabidela*

*Carne de Balchão* (Pork with shrimp paste)

Veal Tongue with White Sauce

Potato Chops

Beef Cutlets

Beef Croquettes

Pork *Vindalho* – *pictured on page 68*

*Chouriço*

Beef Roll

*Bife em Sangue (*Pan-broiled Steak)

*Empada de Carne de Porco* (Pork Pie)

*Lingua Salgada* (Salted Beef Tongue)

## C. Meats and Poultry

Chicken and pork are the main meats used in Goan cooking for special occasions. Beef is usually of poor quality and does not appear generally in Goan festive menus. Beef was, however, the daily fare in many Goan households.

The more pungent meat dishes--*xacuti*, chicken curry, *sarapatel*, *cabidela,* and pork *vindalho*, -- which generally have some form of rice preparation as an accompaniment, are usually served only at lunch.

At dinner, the blander dishes, which are eaten with bread, are served. Included are, for example, potato chops, cutlets, veal tongue.

The meat dish would be the second course of a dinner which would include a light soup and end with fruit or a light dessert.

*Xacuti*, *sarapatel* and *cabidela*, along with *chouriço* would be regular features of festive menus.

### *Xacuti* – pictured on page 67

This dish is supposed to be of Muslim origin because the main ingredient is goat (cabrito) or mutton.

*Ingredients*                                         Preparation time: 35 minutes
                                                     Cooking time: 45 minutes

1 lb goat, mutton, lamb, (or even, beef or chicken), cubed or cut in small pieces
Salt to taste
15 peppercorns
1 tablespoon cumin seeds
7 large red chilies
12 cloves garlic
1 teaspoon turmeric
8 cloves
2 tablespoons coriander powder
1 tablespoon poppy seeds
2 tablespoons vegetable oil
1 medium onion, cut fine
½ grated coconut (see "Useful Tips" section)
½ cup water
2 medium onions, cut coarse
2 small potatoes, peeled and cubed
Salt to taste

*Preparation*
1. Trim the meat of fat, salt to taste and set aside.
2. Roast the spices for 3 minutes and then grind to make a *masala*.

3. Heat the oil and lightly fry the fine cut onion.
4. Add the *masala* and the coconut and mix well while cooking for 5 minutes.
5. Add the meat and mix in well with the spices, and cook over low heat until juices are dry.
6. Add the water, coarsely cut onions and potatoes, and cook for 15-20 minutes.
7. Serve hot with *oddes/puris* (see Section "Rice and Breads") or boiled/steamed rice.

**Chicken Curry** – *pictured on page 67*

*Ingredients*

Preparation time: 25 minutes
Cooking time: 45 minutes

3 tablespoons oil
2 medium onions sliced
1 teaspoon turmeric
¼ inch ginger
8 cloves of garlic, finely sliced
½ teaspoon poppy seeds
1 teaspoon red chili powder
1 tablespoon cumin seeds
2 tablespoons coriander
1 tablespoon tamarind juice (see "Useful Tips" section)
1 cup coconut milk (see "Useful Tips" section)
4 lb chicken parts
Salt to taste

*Preparation*
1. Heat the oil and fry the onions until golden.
2. Add the spices and tamarind juice and mix thoroughly.
3. Add the chicken and mix with the spices.
4. Add the coconut milk, and water if necessary, and cook for about 30 minutes, or until chicken is tender.
5. Serve hot with boiled/steamed rice.

***Sarapatel*** – *pictured on page 68*

*Ingredients*

Preparation time: 40 minutes
Cooking time: 140 minutes

*Cook until tender*
   2 lb pork cut in small pieces
   ½ lb pig's liver cut in small pieces
   1 tablespoon salt
   1½ teaspoons turmeric
   6 cups water

*Grind until fine:*
- 2 teaspoons tamarind juice (see "Useful Tips" section)
- 5 tablespoons white vinegar
- 2 oz red chilies
- 1 tablespoon cumin powder
- 30 cloves of garlic
- 1 teaspoon black pepper

2 tablespoons vegetable oil
3 long green chilies, cut fine
2 large onions, cut fine
1 cup pig's blood (optional)
½ cup white vinegar, if pig's blood is used
Sugar to taste

*Preparation*
1. Cook the pork meat and liver pieces with the salt and turmeric for approximately 20 minutes.
2. Remove the meat from the stock and set aside.
3. To the stock, add the ground spices.
4. Cook the mixture, bringing it to a boil, for 15 minutes.
5. In a frying pan, heat 1 tablespoon vegetable oil, and fry the meat for 15 minutes until brown. Remove the meat and set aside.
6. In the same frying pan, heat the remaining oil and fry the onions until golden.
7. If blood is available, boil it with ½ cup of white vinegar and salt, until the blood is dry. Add to the fried onions and fry. (This step is optional).
8. Add the meat, onions, and blood (optional), to the gravy mixture in (4) above.
9. Cook the mixture for an additional 10-15 minutes.
10. Taste the gravy; if pungent, add a bit of sugar.

### Cabidela

*Ingredients*

Preparation time: 35 minutes
Cooking time: 45 minutes

4 lb duck meat, cut in small pieces
2 tablespoons vegetable oil
4 medium onions, cut fine
½ teaspoon finely cut ginger
1 teaspoon finely cut garlic
1 green (jalapeno or serrano) chili, finely cut
¼ teaspoon turmeric
1½ teaspoons tamarind juice (see "Useful Tips" section)
¼ teaspoon black pepper
¼ teaspoon cumin powder
½ cup white vinegar
½ cup duck blood (optional)
Sugar to taste

*Preparation*
1. Fry the meat in 2 tablespoons of vegetable oil. Remove and set aside.
2. In the same pan, fry the onions in the same oil.
3. Add the ginger, garlic, chili, turmeric and tamarind juice.
4. To this liquid, add the black pepper and cumin.
5. Add the meat and cook until done.
6. Optionally, add the blood mixed with ¼ cup of vinegar, and cook for 10 minutes.
7. Taste. If more vinegar is needed, add as required, and sugar to taste.

*Note:* This dish can also be prepared by substituting duck meat with chicken or suckling pig.

### *Carne de Balchão*
(Pork with shrimp paste)

*Ingredients*

Preparation time: 25 minutes
Cooking time: 30 minutes

2 lb pork, with fat, cut in large cubes
2 large onions, coarsely chopped

*Grind into a fine paste*
    2 heaping tablespoons hot red chili powder
    1 large clove garlic, coarsely cut
    2 teaspoons cumin powder
    10 peppercorns
    ¼ inch fresh ginger, cut coarsely
    ¼ teaspoon turmeric
    ½ cup white vinegar

3 or 4 tablespoons *balchão* shrimp sauce or dried shrimp (found in Thai grocery stores)
2 cups water
Salt and white vinegar to taste

*Preparation*
1. Fry the meat in its own fat, in a large pan.
2. Add the onions and fry until golden.
3. When the onions soften, add the spices ground with the vinegar, and the *balchão* mixture.
4. Transfer the contents to a 10- inch saucepan, add 2 cups of water, and cook until meat is soft.
5. Taste. Add more salt and vinegar if needed.
6. Serve with white rice.

## Veal Tongue with White Sauce

*Ingredients*

Preparation time: 40 minutes
Cooking time: pressure cooker:
30 minutes / stove top: 2 hours

*For the tongue*
1 veal tongue cleaned
2 cups water
1 large onion, coarsely chopped
4 cloves
2 bay leaves
1 teaspoon salt
1 stick cinnamon
2 cloves garlic

*For the white sauce*
2 medium onions, finely cut
10 cloves garlic mashed
½ teaspoon black pepper
2 tablespoons vegetable oil
¾ cup milk

*Preparation*
1. Place tongue in a pressure cooker, with water, chopped onion, and spices. Place on stove and cook until the pressure cooker whistles. Turn the heat down to low and cook for approximately 30 minutes.
2. If a pressure cooker is not available, cover the tongue with water, the onion and spices and cook over the stove for approximately 2 hours, until the tongue is tender when pierced with a fork.
3. Remove the tongue. Let it cool. Peel the skin from the tongue. Refrigerate the stock.
4. White sauce: Fry onions, garlic and black pepper in oil for about one minute. Add 1 cup of degreased tongue stock. Add ¾ cup of milk. Cook on low heat for 15 minutes.
5. Cut tongue in thin slices and place in a serving dish. Cover tongue with the white sauce.
6. Serve hot with crunchy bread rolls.

## Potato Chops

*Ingredients*

Preparation time: 25 minutes
Cooking time: 20 minutes

6 large potatoes
Salt to taste
⅛ cup milk
1 teaspoon butter
1 lb lean ground beef
1 medium onion, finely chopped

1 tomato finely cut
2 cloves garlic, finely chopped
¼ inch ginger, finely chopped
¼ teaspoon red chili powder
1 small green chili, finely sliced
¼ teaspoon turmeric
½ teaspoon tamarind juice
1 egg, lightly beaten
Bread crumbs
Vegetable oil for frying

*Preparation*
1. Boil the potatoes, add salt, milk and butter, and mash them.
2. Divide into eight equal potato balls.
3. Mold in the palm of the hand into an oval or round shape.
4. Make a depression at the top of each potato round or oval. Set aside.
5. In a frying pan, mix together the ground beef with the onion, tomato and all the spices and fry well in its own oil. If necessary, add a little bit of water and cover while cooking. When the mixture is relatively dry, remove it from the fire.
6. Take spoonfuls of the mixture and fill the depression in each one of the potato rounds.
7. Cover the mixture with some mashed potato.
8. Brush each potato round with beaten egg, and lightly coat with bread crumbs.
9. Fry in hot oil on both sides.
10. Serve hot.

## Beef Cutlets

*Ingredients*  Preparation time: 2 days
Cooking time: 20 minutes

1 lb boneless beef
2 tablespoons vegetable or olive oil
1 teaspoon sliced garlic
2 teaspoons black pepper
½ teaspoon salt
Juice of half a lemon
1 bunch fresh coriander, sliced
2 green (jalapeno or serrano) chilies, cut very fine
2 medium onions, cut very fine
3 eggs lightly beaten
2 tablespoons for frying
Bread crumbs

*Preparation*
1. Marinate the meat (cut in 3 inch round pieces) with the oil, garlic, pepper, salt and lemon. With a meat hammer, pound the meat to flatten it.

2. Mix in the oil, the coriander, chilies, and onions and marinate for approximately two days in the refrigerator, stirring the mixture a number of times during the day.
3. On the serving day, dip each cutlet in egg mixture.
4. Heat 2 tablespoons of oil in a frying pan and brown each cutlet on both sides.
5. Serve hot.

## Beef Croquettes

*Ingredients*

Preparation time: 45 minutes
Cooking time: 15 minutes

*Grind into a fine paste*
 2 red chilies
 4 peppercorns
 ½ inch piece ginger, sliced
 4 cloves garlic, chopped
 1 teaspoon coriander seeds
 4 whole cloves
 ½ teaspoon ground cinnamon
 1 teaspoon cumin
 1 tablespoon tamarind juice (see "Useful Tips" section)

1 lb beef, cut into 2 inch cubes
1½ cups water
1 sliced onion
1 large spicy Goa sausage or hot chorizo (cooked)
1 or 2 green (jalapeno or serrano) chilies, depending on desired piquancy
1 large slice of bread
1 whole egg
Salt and pepper, to taste
White vinegar, if necessary
Flour for rolling croquettes (about 4 tablespoons)
1 whole egg, lightly beaten
¾ or ½ cup breadcrumbs
2 ½ - 3 cups of oil for deep frying

*Preparation*
1. Apply the spice paste to meat and let it stand for 15 minutes.
2. Cook the meat in a covered saucepan with 1 ½ cups of water, until the meat is tender. Uncover the pan, raise the heat to medium high to dry out the excess moisture. Cool.
3. Grind the meat into a fine paste with the sliced onion, 1 large spicy Goa sausage or chorizo (cooked), green chilies and the slice of bread.
4. Mix the ground mixture with a whole egg, salt, pepper and a little vinegar, if necessary.
5. Form into 2 inch cylindrical rolls. Roll in flour.
6. Dip in beaten egg and roll in breadcrumbs.
7. Refrigerate for about one hour
8. Deep fry in hot oil. Serve hot.

## Pork *Vindalho* – *pictured on page 68*

*Ingredients*

Preparation time: 20 minutes
plus 4-6 hours for marinade
Cooking time: 55 minutes

1 teaspoon tamarind juice (see "Useful Tips" section)
1 teaspoon cumin powder
6 cloves garlic, chopped
1 inch of ginger, finely chopped
3 peppercorns
1 teaspoon turmeric
25 red chilies, with seeds removed
¼ cup white vinegar
3 lb pork, cut into one-inch pieces
Water sufficient to cover meat
8 small onions

*Preparation*
1. Grind the spices with the vinegar to form a paste or *masala/mirem*.
2. Apply to the pork as a marinade, and refrigerate in a ceramic container for 4 to 6 hours.
3. Add enough water to cover the meat. Add the onions.
4. Bring to a boil. Cook on a low flame until the meat is tender.
5. Serve hot with rice or bread.

## *Chouriço*
### (Sausage)

Sausages were usually filled into skins made from cleaned, washed and dried guts. Nowadays, artificial casings are available. Traditionally in Goa after the sausages are ready, they are sun dried or smoked near the fireplace. As this is a laborious process, we offer the alternative of bottling and refrigerating the *chouriço*/sausage meat preparation and boiling it, serving it as needed.

*Ingredients*

Preparation time: 8 days
Cooking time: 10 minutes

½ lb saltpetre
5 lb boneless fatty pork, cut in strips
5 cloves garlic
¼ lb chili powder
1 teaspoon black pepper
1½ tablespoons turmeric
1 teaspoon cumin
1 tablespoon ginger
4 cups white vinegar
1 cup palm *feni (optional)*

*Preparation*
1. Apply ¼ pound of saltpetre to the meat, and keep it under a heavy weight for four hours. Drain the liquid that comes out of the meat.
2. Apply another ¼ pound of saltpetre and again place the meat under a heavy weight, this time for 48 hours.
3. On the third day, drain all the liquid. Wipe the meat with a clean cloth. Cut the meat in small cubes and keep in a dry container that has a cover.
4. Grind the spices and mix them well with the meat, adding the vinegar and *feni (optional)*, little by little while mixing.
5. Seal the jar tightly. Let the meat marinate in a refrigerator for 6 days.
6. Take out the quantity necessary for serving from the jar. Re-seal the jar tightly.
7. Cook the meat in a very small quantity of water and its own fat. Serve hot. A sliced onion may be added.

*Note:* In the US, saltpetre is only available from chemical laboratories supply stores. It is not sold retail.

## Beef Roll

*Ingredients* (6 to 8 servings)

Preparation time: 45 minutes plus marination time
Cooking time: 1 ½ - 2 hours

1 Goa sausage or spicy Mexican/Spanish chorizo
2 lb flank steak
¼ teaspoon salt
1/3 teaspoon black pepper
3 or 4 hardboiled eggs
2 tablespoons butter
½ cup water or beef bouillon
String for tying the beef roll

*Preparation*
1. Cook the sausage as indicated under "Chouriço". Remove the casing as only the stuffing will be used together with the cooked onion.
2. Sprinkle the salt and pepper on the steak. Pound it lightly with a meat hammer. Allow to marinate for about 1 hour in the refrigerator.
3. Remove from the refrigerator. Spread the sausage meat and onion in a thin layer on the meat. Place the hardboiled eggs, whole, tightly against each other along the edge of the longest side of the steak (depending on the length of the steak, 3 or 4 eggs will be required). To facilitate the process, you may wish to fasten the eggs in place with a wooden skewer or a long wooden toothpick.
4. Roll the meat lengthwise, so that the eggs will not be squeezed out during cooking.
5. In a heavy cast-iron skillet, melt the butter and brown the roll on all the sides.
6. Place the roll in a baking dish, pour over it the water or bouillon, cover tightly, and bake in a 300°F oven until done (about 1 ½ - 2 hours).
7. To serve, cut into one-inch slices and serve with the degreased pan drippings. This dish looks very attractive as the four "layers" are visible – the brown of the meat, the red of the sausage, the white and then the yellow of the egg.

## *Bife em Sangue*
(Pan-Broiled Steak)

This dish is very simple, quick and easy, but it does require a good cut of beef. The tenderer rib end (rib-eye steak) or tenderloin are best for this entrée.

*Ingredients (6 servings)*

Preparation time: 15 minutes
plus marinating time
Cooking time: 20 minutes

2 lb boneless steak, sliced into 1 ½ slices
1 tablespoon lemon juice
½ teaspoon black pepper
1½ tablespoons butter
1 tablespoon olive oil
½ tablespoon flour
½ cup beef bouillon

*Preparation*
1. Lightly pound the beef slices. Season with the lemon juice and black pepper and let it stand for about an hour in the refrigerator.
2. Combine the butter and olive oil in a skillet, over moderately high heat.
3. When the butter/oil is hot (not smoking) place the steak pieces comfortably in the pan. (Do not overcook them).
4. When tiny beads of blood surface to the top, turn the slices and cook them just for a minute or two longer. These slices should come out medium rare.
5. Repeat the process with the remaining slices.
6. Place the meat on a platter. Into a skillet, put the flour and together with the pan drippings make a paste. Quickly add the bouillon, and stirring continually, produce a nice smooth sauce.
7. Pour the sauce over the steaks, and serve immediately.

## *Empada de Carne de Porco*
(Pork Pie)

*Ingredients*

Preparation time: 25 minutes
Cooking time: 60 minutes

2 tablespoons vegetable oil
1 large onion sliced fine
8 cloves
1 tablespoon cumin powder
½ teaspoon black pepper
¼ teaspoon turmeric powder (or a pinch of saffron)
1 tablespoon white vinegar
1 lb pork, cut in cubes
2 teaspoons tamarind juice (see "Useful Tips" section)
½ teaspoon salt
1 cup water
2 boiled eggs

Bread crumbs
1 tablespoon butter

*Preparation*
1. Heat the oil and lightly fry the sliced onions.
2. Grind the spices in vinegar and tamarind juice. Add the spices to the onion and fry for 5 minutes, mixing well.
3. Add the meat, salt, and water; cook on low heat until meat is cooked (about 30 minutes).
4. Spread the cooked meat in a pie dish. Top with sliced boiled eggs, a heavy layer of bread crumbs, gravy from the meat, and 1 tablespoon of butter.
5. Bake in an oven at low heat (250°F) until the crust turns light brown (about 20 minutes).
6. Serve hot.

## Lingua Salgada
(Salted Beef Tongue)

*Ingredients*

Preparation time: 20 minutes plus marinating time
Cooking time: 1 hour in pressure cooker
2 ½ to 3 hours on top of stove

2 to 2 ½ lb beef tongue
½ teaspoon saltpetre (available in chemical supply stores)
3 tablespoons salt (coarse is best)
Juice of 1 medium size sour lime
½ cup tightly packed brown sugar
1 cup water

*Preparation*
1. Cook the tongue for 2 minutes in boiling water. Take off the flame and remove the skin.
2. Clean the tongue under running water and dry it.
3. Prick the tongue thoroughly with a sturdy fork and coat it with the saltpetre and let it marinate for ½ hour.
4. In a separate bowl mix together 3 tablespoons salt, lime juice and the brown sugar.
5. Place the tongue in the bowl and coat it with the salt- lime juice – brown sugar mixture and let it marinate in the refrigerator for 8 days. The tongue has to be turned and pricked every day so that it absorbs the mixture.
6. Remove from the refrigerator on the 8th day and cook the tongue along with the marinating juice and 1 cup of water in a pressure cooker for an hour.
7. Remove the tongue from the liquid.
8. Slice the tongue at a diagonal angle in fine slices and serve cold with rice or salad.

*Note:* If cooked on top of the stove, the cooking time will be 2 ½ to 3 hours on a very low flame, until tongue is fork tender. The marinade plus water should be at least 3 cups. The liquid should rise so as to reach the half-point level of the tongue. This salted tongue keeps well in the refrigerator for a week. It also freezes well, but should be used within a month.

*Xacuti*

**Chicken Curry**

*Sarapatel and Sannas*

*Pork Vindalho*

## D. Vegetables and Eggs

*Dudhi* (Pumpkin)
*Tantiam Koddi* (Egg Curry)
Potato *Bhaji*
Spinach I
Spinach II
*Vadde Bhaji*
Baked Spinach Casserole
Okra I
Okra II
Okra with Grated Coconut
*Brinjal* (Eggplant) Casserole
*Brinjal Botha* (Pureed Eggplant)
Layered *Brinjal* (Eggplant) Casserole with Coconut Sauce

## D. Vegetables and Eggs

Goan vegetable dishes are similar to those in coastal southern India.

Vegetables were generally grown in home gardens and were seasonal. The principal vegetables that were commonly available in earlier times were okra, spinach (red and green varieties) (*bhaji*), eggplant *(brinjal)*, yellow and white pumpkin *(dudhi)*, tomatoes, cucumber, white radish (*mooli*), small gherkins *(tendlim)*, bitter gourd *(karela)*, bread fruit, drumsticks *(sehjana ki phali*), were the principal vegetables that were commonly available. Nowadays, all vegetables are available as they are brought from neighboring districts. But, Goan menus, as discussed earlier, also include asparagus soup, using canned asparagus imported from Europe.

As in the case of Western menus, vegetables were served as accompaniments to fish and meat dishes, in particular those that are not curried or heavily spiced.

Egg curry is easy to prepare and can either be served with rice, or as an additional curried dish. It has its *aficionados*.

### *Dudhi*
(Pumpkin)

*Ingredients* (6 servings)

Preparation time: 10 minutes
Cooking time: 15 minutes

1 large onion, cut fine
1 tablespoon vegetable oil
6 cloves garlic, cut fine
½ inch ginger, cut fine
½ lb pumpkin
½ cup grated coconut (see "Useful Tips" section)
Salt to taste

*Preparation*
1. Fry the onion in heated oil. Add garlic and ginger. Cook until the onion is golden.
2. Add the pumpkin, grated coconut, and salt to taste.
3. Cover with water and cook until done.

### *Tantiam Koddi*
(Egg Curry)

*Ingredients* (6 servings)

Preparation time: 15 minutes
Cooking time: 25-30 minutes

1 medium onion cut fine
2 tablespoons vegetable oil
4 medium red chilies
4 cloves garlic cut fine

½ teaspoon turmeric
1½ cups thin coconut milk (see "Useful Tips" section)
1 cup thick coconut milk
6 hard-boiled eggs, cut in half

*Preparation*
1. Fry the onion in oil. Add and fry the other spices.
2. Add the thin coconut milk and cook for 10 minutes.
3. Add the thick coconut milk and cook for 5 minutes.
4. Add the eggs and cook covered for 10 minutes. Add water, if necessary.

## Potato *Bhaji*

*Ingredients* (6 servings)                                  Preparation time: 15 minutes
                                                            Cooking time: 35 minutes

4 large potatoes
Salted water
2 onions finely minced
2 tablespoons vegetable oil
½ teaspoon mustard seeds
Pinch saffron powder (if not available, use turmeric powder)
½ teaspoon of red chili powder
1 or 2 green (jalapeno or serrano) chilies, coarsely chopped
1 bunch coriander (cilantro) leaves (if not available, use parsley and chives), finely cut
Salt to taste

*Preparation*
1. Boil the potatoes in salted water.
2. Cut in 1 inch cubes.
3. Fry the onions until cooked but not brown.
4. Throw in the mustard seeds.
5. When the mustard seeds start to splutter, add saffron powder, red chili powder, cut potatoes, jalapeno peppers and salt to taste.
6. Sprinkle coriander (cilantro) leaves.
7. Serve hot.

*Note:* This mixture is rather dry and tastes better if prepared a day ahead of serving time.

## Spinach I

*Ingredients* (4 servings)                                  Preparation time: 20 minutes
                                                            Cooking time: 20 minutes

1 medium onion, finely cut
1 tablespoon vegetable oil

6 cloves garlic, finely cut
½ teaspoon fresh ground pepper
½ lb fresh spinach cleaned, and cut fine
½ cup coconut milk (see "Useful Tips" section)
4 eggs

*Preparation*
1. Fry the onion in the heated oil, with the garlic and pepper.
2. Add the spinach and mix thoroughly.
3. Cover with coconut milk and cook until spinach is soft.
4. Transfer to an oven-proof dish. Break 4 whole eggs at regular intervals on the surface of the dish, taking care to keep the eggs separate and the egg yolks whole.
5. Cook in oven at 350°F for approximately 15 minutes.
6. Serve hot.

## Spinach II

*Ingredients* (6 servings)  Preparation time: 15 minutes
Cooking time: 20 minutes

2 large bunches fresh spinach or one packet (10 oz) frozen spinach
2 medium onions
2 tablespoons butter or olive oil
1 teaspoon cumin seeds
½ teaspoon red chili powder
½ teaspoon powdered ginger
½ teaspoon salt (or more, if desired)

*Preparation*
1. Clean and wash the fresh spinach. Remove the thick stalks and chop. If using frozen spinach allow it to thaw and squeeze out as much water as possible.
2. Chop the onions very finely.
3. Heat the butter or oil in a skillet and fry the onions until they are soft.
4. Add the cumin seeds, chili powder, and fry for 2 or 3 minutes.
5. Add the prepared spinach and the ginger and cook covered, for 5 minutes.
6. Add the salt and cook uncovered until the liquid is almost all absorbed.
7. Cover and cook on a very low heat until the spinach is cooked, about 5-7 minutes.

## *Vadde Bhaji*

The *vadde bhaji* dish, uses the leaves of a home-grown creeper which has flat round leaves, that is plentiful in Goan gardens. The closest match in the US would be collard greens or spinach.

*Ingredients* (6 servings)  Preparation time: 25 minutes
Cooking time: 25 minutes

1 lb fresh greens
2 medium sized onions

½ teaspoon ginger paste (see "Useful Tips" section)
½ teaspoon garlic paste (see "Useful Tips" section)
½ cup *masoor dal* (red lentils)
2 tablespoons oil
2 cups (16 oz) fresh coconut milk (see "Useful Tips" section). A commercial 14 oz can of coconut milk may be used as a substitute
½ cup small prawns, peeled, cleaned and deveined
1 ½ teaspoons salt

*Preparation*
1. Wash the greens. Remove tough stalks. Cut into fine strips.
2. Finely chop the onions and set aside.
3. Wash the lentils in cold water until the water runs clear. Allow to soak until needed. Drain before use.
4. In a saucepan, on medium heat, heat the oil and sauté the onions until they are soft.
5. Add the ginger and garlic paste and cook for about one minute.
6. Add the chopped greens.
7. Add the drained lentils and cook for 2 minutes longer.
8. Add 1 cup coconut milk and boil over a high flame for about 15 minutes.
9. Add 2$^{nd}$ cup of coconut milk and allow boiling for 5 additional minutes.
10. Add the prawns and the salt, and cook for 5 more minutes until the prawns turn pink.
11. Remove from the stove and serve hot.

## Baked Spinach Casserole

*Ingredients* (6 servings)                                  Preparation time: 30 minutes
                                                            Cooking time: 30 minutes

1 lb spinach (the frozen chopped variety is suitable for this recipe)
1 cup water
3 tablespoons flour
2 cups milk
4 tablespoons grated cheese
1 teaspoon salt
1 tablespoon butter
1 egg
Butter for greasing dish

*Preparation*
1. Place the spinach (chopped, if fresh; thawed, if frozen) in a saucepan with 1 cup of water. Boil on high heat for 2 minutes. Drain into a colander.
2. Return the spinach to the pan, and cook on a low flame until all the water evaporates.
3. In a small quart saucepan, make a sauce as follows:
    a. Roast the flour for 2 or 3 minutes over a low flame.
    b. Add 2 cups milk and stir until the mixture is very smooth.
    c. Add 3 tablespoons of grated cheese, salt and butter and mix well.

d. Raise the heat to medium high and cook the sauce, stirring continually, to avoid lumps, until the mixture is very thick.
e. Remove from the heat and set aside.
4. Beat the egg well in a small bowl, and add ½ of it to the sauce, mixing well. Combine the sauce and the spinach.
5. Generously butter the inside of an oven-proof casserole dish and place the mixture in the dish. Coat the top with the remainder of the egg and sprinkle with the remaining 1 tablespoon of grated cheese.
6. Preheat the oven to 325°F. Bake for 15 minutes.
7. Serve hot.

## Okra I

Okra grows plentifully in Goa during the monsoon, and so okra was featured regularly at meals throughout the season.

*Ingredients* (6 servings)　　　　　　　　　　　　　　　　Preparation time: 15 minutes
　　　　　　　　　　　　　　　　　　　　　　　　　　　Cooking time: 20 minutes

1 lb okra
3 tablespoons oil
2 teaspoons red chili powder
½ teaspoon ginger paste & ½ teaspoon garlic paste (see "Useful Tips" section)
2 tablespoons white vinegar
½ tablespoon sugar
1 teaspoon salt

*Preparation*
1. Wash and dry the okra. Cut off and discard the stems and the fine tips. Slice the okra into rounds about ½ inch thick.
2. Heat the oil in a saucepan over medium high heat, toss in the sliced okra and then lower the flame.
3. Add the chili powder, the ginger and garlic pastes, the vinegar, sugar and salt. Stir well to coat the okra.
4. Cook for 20 minutes, stirring occasionally.
5. Serve hot.

## Okra II

*Ingredients* (6 servings)　　　　　　　　　　　　　　　　Preparation time: 20 minutes
　　　　　　　　　　　　　　　　　　　　　　　　　　　Cooking time: 20 minutes

1 tablespoon vegetable oil
1 onion cut in five pieces
2 cloves garlic cut fine
½ inch fresh ginger, cut fine

1 tomato, cut fine
½ cup grated coconut (see "Useful Tips" section)
½ lb okra cut in rounds, soaked in water
Water for cooking okra
2 green (jalapeno or serrano) chilies, cut fine
1 cup cooked prawns (optional)

*Preparation*
1. Fry the onion in heated oil until golden.
2. Add the garlic, ginger, tomato, and grated coconut, mix well and fry.
3. Add the drained okra and green chilies. Cover with water and cook until okra is tender.
4. 1 cup of cooked prawns can be added to this dish.
5. Serve hot.

## Okra with Grated Coconut

*Ingredients* (6 servings)  Preparation time: 35 minutes
Cooking time: 25 minutes

½ lb okra
1 cup grated coconut (see "Useful Tips" section)
½ to ¾ teaspoon red chili powder
3 cloves of garlic, coarsely chopped
¼ teaspoon black peppercorns
¼ teaspoon coriander seeds
½ teaspoon cumin seeds
1 ½ cups hot water
1 ½ tablespoons cooking oil
1 medium sized onion (sliced fine)
¼ teaspoon turmeric powder
8 to 10 medium-size prawns, peeled and deveined
½ teaspoon salt
½ teaspoon tamarind juice (see "Useful Tips" section)
1 green (jalapeno or serrano) chili, slit lengthwise and de-seeded

*Preparation*
1. Wash and dry the okra. Cut off and discard the stems and the fine tips. Cut into ¾ inch rounds.
2. In a blender, combine the coconut with the chili powder, garlic, peppercorns, coriander seeds, cumin seeds, and ½ cup hot water and liquefy. Extract the juice from the mixture by passing it through a fine sieve. The yield should be approximately ½ cup of relatively thick coconut juice. Repeat the process by combining the residue with 1 cup of hot water. After straining the liquid, yield of a thinner coconut milk should be approximately 1 cup. Keep the two types of coconut milk in separate containers.
3. Heat the oil in a saucepan and sauté the onion slices until translucent. Add the turmeric powder and fry for about 2 minutes.

4. Add the prawns and sauté until the prawns turn pink. Add the thin coconut milk and allow to come to a boil. Lower the heat and throw in the okra bits, the salt and the tamarind juice. Stir.
5. Cover and cook till almost dry (about 15 minutes).
6. Add the thick coconut milk, and the green chili and simmer an additional 6 minutes. Remove the chili.
7. Serve hot.

## *Brinjal* (Eggplant) Casserole

*Ingredients* (6 servings)

Preparation time: 30 minutes
Cooking time: 25 minutes

1 lb eggplant *(brinjal)*
1 teaspoon salt
2 tablespoons oil (additional oil, if needed)
4 medium size onions, chopped fine
1 teaspoon ground cumin
2 teaspoons *garam masala* (found in Asian groceries)
1 teaspoon ginger paste (see "Useful Tips" section)
1 teaspoon garlic paste (see "Useful Tips" section)
1 ½ teaspoons sugar
2 tablespoons white vinegar
Butter to grease the serving dish
1 egg, well-beaten

*Preparation*
1. Peel the eggplant. Dice into 1 inch cubes. Season with salt and set aside.
2. In a skillet, heat the oil, and sauté the onions until soft. Remove the onions from the pan and set aside.
3. In the same skillet, adding a little more oil if necessary, sauté the eggplant cubes, tossing them frequently, for about 5 minutes.
4. Remove from the pan, leaving as much oil in the pan as possible.
5. Add a little more oil, if necessary, and add the cumin, *garam masala*, ginger and garlic pastes, sugar and vinegar.
6. Return the onions and brinjal to the pan and mix well.
7. Grease an oven proof casserole with butter, pack the prepared mixture into the casserole, coat the top with a well-beaten egg and bake in a 350°F oven for 25 minutes.
8. Serve hot.

### *Brinjal Botha*
(Pureed Eggplant)

*Ingredients* (6 servings)

Preparation time: 10 minutes
Cooking time: 50 minutes

1 eggplant (about 8 oz)
2 tablespoons oil
½ teaspoon white vinegar
¼ - ½ teaspoon salt
1 green (jalapeno or serrano) chili, de-seeded and finely minced

*Preparation*
1. Apply oil to the surface of the eggplant and cut 6 deep gashes on to the surface.
2. Wrap in aluminum foil and bake in a 400°F oven for approximately 45 minutes.
3. Allow to cool. Cut off the caps at either end, peel. Discard caps and skin.
4. Chop the pulp coarsely with a potato masher. Sprinkle with the vinegar and salt, add the chili and mix well.
5. Serve at room temperature.

### Layered *Brinjal* (Eggplant) Casserole with Coconut Sauce

*Ingredients* (6 servings)

Preparation time: 40 minutes
plus weighting time
Cooking time: 25 minutes

1 lb *brinjal* (eggplant)
Juice of half a lemon
1 ½ teaspoons coarse salt
Flour for dredging
2 tablespoons oil
2 large onions, finely minced
6 cloves garlic, finely minced
¼ lb medium size prawns, cleaned and deveined
3 medium size tomatoes (skinned, seeded and cut into semicircular slices)
2 tablespoons water
1 ¼ cups thick coconut milk (see "Useful Tips" section)
Salt to taste
¼ teaspoon black pepper
½ cup grated cheese

*Preparation*
1. Cut off the stalks and caps from the eggplant and slice into ¼ inch slices. Rub the slices with lemon juice (you may use a pastry brush very lightly) to prevent discoloration. Toss them with the coarse salt. Stack the slices in a plastic or glass container; weigh them down with a heavy object of your choice, for at least an hour. Drain off excess water.

2. Dredge the slices in the flour on both sides and fry them in shallow hot oil, a few at a time, turning them frequently until they are golden and cooked through. Drain on absorbent paper towels.
3. In a saucepan, heat 2 tablespoons of oil, sauté the minced onions until translucent. Add the minced garlic and fry for one or two minutes (do not let the garlic burn, as it will taste bitter).
4. Add the prawns and sauté till it turns pink.
5. Add slices of tomatoes and 2 tablespoons of water.
6. Cover and cook for about 10 minutes, until the tomatoes are soft and the moisture evaporates.
7. Add the coconut milk, salt and pepper and simmer gently for an additional 6 minutes, until the sauce is slightly condensed.
8. Grease an ovenproof casserole. Place the eggplant slices in a layer at the bottom, top it with sauce. Repeat the process until you end with a layer of sauce on the top. Sprinkle the grated cheese on top.
9. Bake for 15 minutes in a preheated 400°F oven, to blend the flavors and brown the top.
10. Serve hot.

## E. Rice and Breads

*Basmati* Rice (Steamed Long-grain Rice)

*Arroz Refugado* – *pictured on page 84*

*Congee (Pez)*

*Arroz Arabe*

*Sannas (*Goan *Idlis)* – *pictured on page 68*

Green *Pulao* – *pictured on page 84*

*Oddes* (*Puris*)

*Açorda de Pão*

## Rice and Breads

These are accompaniments to fish, seafood and meat dishes. Some of them are necessary combinations: *xacuti* and *oddes* (*puris*) or *sarapatel* and *sannas*. The others can accompany a variety of dishes.

A dish of *arroz refugado*, with its saffron colored rice surrounded by sliced boiled eggs, *chouriços* and black and green olives makes a colorful centerpiece for a festive table, and is a staple at most dinners.

*Congee*, which is also known in Chinese Malay and Malaysian cooking, is generally served at breakfast (see section on "Soups").

### *Basmati Rice*
(Steamed Long-Grain Rice)

*Ingredients* (2 servings)

Preparation time: 5 minutes
Cooking time: 20 minutes

1 cup *basmati* rice
2 cups water
Salt to taste

*Preparation*
1. Wash the rice thoroughly to remove impurities and starch.
2. Put 2 cups of water in a pot and bring to boil.
3. Add rice and salt, and stir lightly with a fork to separate grains.
4. Cover the pot and cook at low heat until the rice is cooked (*al dente* or the grains are separate). Any remaining water should be poured out. Avoid making the rice sticky.

### *Arroz Refugado* – pictured on page 84

*Ingredients* (6 servings)

Preparation time: 20 minutes
Cooking time: 25-30 minutes

2 cups of *basmati* rice
3 tablespoons vegetable oil
1 large onion, very finely sliced
¼ teaspoon turmeric or pinch saffron
3 cups of chicken or beef stock (or 2 bouillon cubes diluted in boiling water)
4 cloves
2½ strips of bacon
1 teaspoon salt

Garnish: 2 small boiled potatoes, 2 boiled eggs, 4-inch piece of cooked *chouriço*, and 20-30 cooked fresh green peas.

*Preparation*
1. Wash the rice and set aside.
2. Heat the oil and fry the onion until golden. Add the turmeric (or saffron) and mix well.
3. Add the stock, cloves and bacon and boil for 5 minutes.
4. Add the rice and salt.
5. Cover the pot and cook on low heat for 25-30 minutes.
6. Place on a platter and garnish with sliced boiled eggs, sliced boiled potatoes, chouriço, and green peas.

## ***Congee***
*(Pez)*

*Ingredients* (4 servings)                                    Preparation time: 5 minutes
                                                              Cooking time: 30-35 minutes

2 cups rice
10 cups water
Salt to taste

*Preparation*
1. Wash rice and set aside.
2. Bring water to boil and add rice and salt.
3. Cook on low heat until rice is cooked.
4. Serve rice with the water in soup bowls.

Accompaniments include condensed shrimp curry, green mango pickled in salt water, and pickled fish.

## ***Arroz Arabe***

*Ingredients* (8 - 10 servings)                               Preparation time: 15 minutes
                                                              Cooking time: 25-30 minutes

4 cups *basmati* rice
1 small chicken
4 cups water
4 medium onions (3 sliced fine and 1 whole)
Salt to taste
4 tablespoons vegetable oil
2 oz sliced almonds
4 oz raisins

*Preparation*
1. Wash the rice and set aside.
2. Boil the chicken in 4 cups of water, with 1 whole onion and salt.
3. When the water has been reduced to 3 cups remove the chicken and slice it into pieces.
4. In a saucepan, heat 3 tablespoons of the oil and fry the rice.

5. Add the chicken stock and chicken pieces and cook until done (about 25 minutes).
6. In a separate frying pan, heat 1 tablespoon of vegetable oil and fry the sliced onions, almonds, and raisins until lightly brown.
7. Put the rice in a serving platter and garnish with the fried onions, almonds and raisins.
8. Serve hot.

### *Sannas* – *pictured on page 68*
### (Goan *Idlis*)

*Ingredients* (4 servings)

Preparation time: 1 day
Cooking time: 30 minutes

2 cups *basmati* rice
1 grated coconut (see "Useful Tips" section)
1 tablespoon sugar
2 cups palm toddy (or 2 teaspoons of yeast)
Salt to taste

*Preparation*
1. Wash and soak the rice overnight.
2. Grind the rice on the next day. Also grate and grind the coconut fine.
3. Mix, the ground rice, coconut, sugar, toddy (or yeast) and salt to make a thick batter.
4. Put in a large covered bowl in a warm place to allow fermentation of the mixture, for about 3 hours, to about twice its volume.
5. Pour the mixture into round medium-size (large size muffin) molds.
6. Steam the molds for about 20 minutes in a steamer. [In Goa, a special steamer, called a *sanna kopro*, made of copper is used.]
7. Insert a toothpick in each mold. If it is dry when extracted, the sannas are ready.
8. Sannas are generally, and especially, served warm with *sarapatel*.

### Green *Pulao* – *pictured on page 84*

*Ingredients* (8 - 10 servings)

Preparation time: 45 minutes
Cooking time: 90 minutes

1 piece of fresh ginger, approximately 2 inches long by ¾ inches wide
16 cloves garlic
1 tablespoon poppy seeds
12 green (jalapeno or serrano) chilies
2 bunches coriander leaves (cilantro)
2 cups *basmati* rice
3 cups water
½ pound butter or *ghee* (clarified butter)
2 medium onions, thinly sliced
1 teaspoon cumin powder
1 - 3 inch long cinnamon stick
1 cup finely grated coconut (see "Useful Tips" section)
1 lb mutton or chicken, cubed

4 cups warm water
Juice of 1 lemon

*Preparation*
1. Grind together the ginger and garlic into a paste. Set aside.
2. Grind together the poppy seeds, the chilies and coriander leaves (cilantro).
3. Boil the rice in the 3 cups of water, until it is almost cooked.
4. Heat the butter or *ghee* and fry the onions a pale brown. Remove the onions from the pan with a slotted spoon, and set aside.
5. Fry in the butter or *ghee*, in sequence, the cumin powder and cinnamon stick, ground ginger-garlic paste, then the chilies-coriander leaves (cilantro)-poppy seed mixture, and finally the grated coconut.
6. Add to the pan, the meat pieces, with 4 cups of warm water, the lemon juice, and cook till the meat is tender.
7. When done, remove pieces of meat and ¾ of the mixture or *masala*.
8. Spread the remainder of the mixture evenly over the bottom of the pan.
9. Place half the rice and onions mixture over the initial layer.
10. Top this layer with the meat and the remainder of the rice.
11. Pour the spicy gravy over the casserole and pour the spicy gravy over the casserole.
12. Bake in a 300°F oven for 45 minutes.
13. Fluff with a fork before serving.

## **Oddes**
(*Puris*)

*Ingredients* (12 servings)

Preparation time: 1 hour
Cooking time: 15 minutes

4 tablespoons flour
1 tablespoon semolina
Pinch of salt
Water to make the dough

*Preparation*
1. Mix ingredients.
2. Knead well. Let stand for ½ hour.
3. Shape into small balls. With a rolling pin, roll into circles and deep fry.
4. Serve very hot with *xacuti* or *bhaji*.

## **Açorda de Pão**

*Ingredients* (4 - 6 servings)

Preparation time: 35 minutes
Cooking time: 25 minutes

20 garlic cloves
5 tablespoons olive oil
1 tablespoon butter
½ lb stale bread, soaked in water
4 lightly beaten eggs

*Preparation*

1. Press the garlic lightly. Then fry it in heated oil. Remove the garlic when lightly brown.
2. Add the butter and bread and cook lightly.
3. Put the eggs over the bread. The mixture is cooked when the eggs are cooked and seen on the top.
4. Serve hot. Optionally, sardines or pieces of hot Portuguese sausages (*Chouriço de Reino*) can be added to this dish.

***Green Pulao***

***Arroz Refugado***

## F. Chutneys and Pickles

*Capsicum* (Bell Pepper) Pickle I
*Capsicum* (Bell Pepper) Pickle II
Lime Pickle
*Tendlim* Pickle (Small Gherkins Pickle)
Mango Chutney
Mango *Miscut* (Spicy Mango Pickle)
*Chepnim Ambli* (Tender Green Mangoes Cured in Salt)
Prawn *Balchão* (Pickled Prawns)
*Brinjal* (Eggplant) Pickle
Apple Chutney
Tomato Chutney
Coriander Leaves (Cilantro) Chutney
Carrot Pickle

## F. Chutneys and Pickles

Chutneys and pickles are usually spicy and often sour. These are served as accompaniments to a meal. One or two teaspoons of a chutney and/or a pickle are usually eaten by each person with a rice and curry dish. I remember my maternal grandfather used to have a side plate with 4 or 5 kinds of chutneys and pickles called in Portuguese "*acepipes*". This is, unavoidably, a habit which I have inherited and indulge in. *Brinjal* (eggplant) pickle is a particular favorite of mine.

### *Capsicum* Pickle I
(Bell Pepper Pickle)

*Ingredients*

Preparation time: 5 minutes
Cooking time: 10 minutes

1 lb *capsicum* (bell peppers), cut in strips
2 teaspoons salt
½ cup water
1 cup white vinegar
2 tablespoons sugar

*Preparation*
1. Salt the *capsicum* (bell pepper) strips and set aside.
2. Boil the water, vinegar, and sugar.
3. Add the *capsicum* (bell pepper) strips and cook only until they change color (5 minutes). Do not let them soften.
4. Cool. Store in a sealed jar.

## *Capsicum* Pickle II
(Bell Pepper Pickle)

*Ingredients*             Preparation time: 20 minutes
Cooking time: 15–20 minutes

Grind to a paste
    2 teaspoons cumin powder
    1 tablespoon coriander powder
    ½ inch of fresh ginger
    6 cloves of garlic
    3 red Kashmiri chilies
    White vinegar for grinding the above into a paste

1 lb *capsicum* (green bell peppers)
½ cup vegetable oil
2 medium size onions, cut fine
1 tablespoon tamarind juice (see "Useful Tips" section)
3 tablespoons sugar
Salt to taste

*Preparation*
1. Grind the spices with the vinegar into a fine paste.
2. Cut the *capsicum* (bell peppers) into fine strips and remove most of the seeds.
3. Heat the oil and fry the onions until brown.
4. Add the ground spices and fry for a few minutes.
5. Add the strips of *capsicum* (bell peppers) and cook for a few minutes.
6. Add the tamarind juice, the sugar and salt.
7. Cook on a slow fire till the *capsicum* (bell peppers) are soft and the mixture is fairly dry.
8. Cool, put in a sealed jar and refrigerate.
9. Serve cold, or a small quantity can be heated, as an accompaniment to any rice and curry dish.

## Lime Pickle

*Ingredients*            Preparation time: 24 hours
Cooking time: 25 minutes

24 limes, cut in quarters
Salt
½ cup water
1 cup white vinegar
2 tablespoons red chili powder
1 cup sugar
5 cloves
Pinch cinnamon powder
10 peppercorns

2 inch piece of ginger, cut in thin slices
1 oz garlic, sliced fine

*Preparation*
1. Salt the limes thoroughly and let them sit for 24 hours.
2. Boil the water, vinegar, red chili powder, and sugar.
3. Add the limes, cloves, cinnamon, peppercorns, ginger, and garlic and cook for 10-15 minutes until the limes are a bit soft.
4. Cool. Store in a sealed jar for 15-20 days to properly season.


### *Tendlim* **Pickle**
(Small Gherkins Pickle)

*Ingredients*

Preparation time: 30 minutes
Cooking time: 50 minutes

1 pound of *tendlim* (small gherkins)
65 Kashmiri red chilies, crushed
3 tablespoons salt
8 cloves garlic finely sliced
3 inches ginger, cut fine
1 ½ teaspoons turmeric powder (or 1 oz of saffron)
1 teaspoon ground cumin
1 cup oil
20 *curry-pak* leaves
3 green (jalapeno or serrano) chilies, coarsely sliced
1 ½ teaspoons black peppercorns, coarsely crushed
¾ teaspoon fenugreek seeds
1 tablespoon mustard seeds
½ cup sugar
1 cup white vinegar

*Preparation*
1. Cut the *tendlim* in rounds, salt and set aside for ½ hour.
2. Grind in vinegar the red chilies, garlic, ginger, ½ teaspoon of turmeric and the cumin.
3. In a large pan, heat the oil. Add the *curry-pak* leaves and green chilies. Cook for 2 minutes.
4. Add the fenugreek seeds, mustard seeds and peppercorns and fry for 2 minutes.
5. Add the sugar and mix until it is dissolved.
6. Add the *tendlim* and cook on low heat for about 25- 30 minutes until the *tendlim* are soft. Do not overcook. The *tendlim* should be soft but firm.
7. Taste and adjust the vinegar, sugar and salt.
8. Cool.
9. Store in a jar for at least 15 days before serving.

# Mango Chutney

*Ingredients*

Preparation time: 60 minutes
Cooking time: 60 minutes

1 oz ginger
1 oz garlic
1 oz red chilies
1⅓ cups white vinegar
3 lb mangoes
3 lb sugar
2 oz slivered almonds
½ lb raisins
Salt to taste

*Preparation*
1. Grind the ginger, garlic, and red chilies with ⅓ cup white vinegar into a *masala*/paste.
2. Slice the mangoes into triangular or rectangular very fine small (about 1 - 1 ½ inch) slices or slivers.
3. Mix together the mangoes and sugar, and cook in a deep pot until the bits are translucent and the mixture has the consistency of a liquid jam.
4. Then add the ground *masala*/paste, almonds, raisins and the rest of the vinegar, and salt to taste, and boil until the mixture is thick.
5. Let cool. Store in tightly sealed jars.


# Mango *Miscut*
(Spicy Mango Pickle)

This is a very pungent mango pickle – not for the faint of tongue or stomach.

*Ingredients*

2 lb raw, very small green mangoes (about 4-5 inches)
1 cup peanut oil
2 inch piece asafetida (to be pounded and powdered) (available in ethnic stores)
3 tablespoons fenugreek seeds
3 tablespoons mustard powder
½ tablespoon turmeric
6 tablespoons salt
6 tablespoons Kashmiri chili powder

*Preparation*
1. Wash and dry the mangoes. Remove seeds and cut into 4 inch pieces.
2. In a pan, heat 1 cup of oil. Add the powdered asafetida and remove from the fire.
3. Add the fenugreek seeds, mustard powder, turmeric, salt, and chili powder to the hot oil and mix well.

4. Let cool without a cover.
   5. Put in the mangoes, mix well and cover.
   6. Next day, mix well again. Third day, mix again and bottle.

### *Chepnim Ambli*
(Tender Green Mangoes Cured in Salt)

*Ingredients*  Preparation time: 1 week
Cooking time: not relevant

50 tender raw green mangoes
6 cups salt
½ teaspoon crushed asafetida (available in ethnic stores)
6 teaspoons turmeric
10 red Kashmiri chilies
Salt for sprinkling

*Preparation*
   1. Take a large earthenware jar and arrange the mangoes in its interior.
   2. Apply all the salt. Sprinkle the asafetida and turmeric, and add the whole red chilies.
   3. Place a heavy weight on the mangoes.
   4. Two or 3 days later turn the mangoes and sprinkle them with additional salt.
   5. Keep in a cool dark place for an additional 3 or 4 days, with weight on the mangoes.
   6. At the end of a week, take out individual mangoes, rinse in clean water, cut into pieces, and serve.

   *Note:* This kind of mango is generally served with *congee* (*pez*).

### Prawn *Balchão*
(Pickled Prawns)

*Ingredients*  Preparation time: 2 weeks
Cooking time: 15 minutes

1 lb of shelled prawns with heads and tails removed
¼ lb salt
4 long red chilies
10 peppercorns
½ teaspoon cumin powder
6 tablespoons white vinegar
6 lime leaves

*Preparation*
   1. Grind the prawns fine, and fry them adding salt.
   2. In a separate skillet, fry (without oil) the chilies, peppercorns, and cumin until lightly brown.

3. When cool, add this mixture to the ground prawns.
4. Put the mixture into a clean jar, insert the lime leaves, and add vinegar.
5. Seal the jar and keep for 7 days.
6. Open the jar and stir the mixture to mix in the vinegar properly with the prawns.
7. Seal the jar tightly and keep for another week.
8. Serve with rice and curry dishes or congee.

## *Brinjal* Pickle
(Eggplant Pickle)

*Ingredients*

Preparation time: 1 hour
Cooking time: 1 ½ - 2 hours

3 lb *brinjals* (small variety)
3 tablespoons salt
2 oz dry red chilies
6 oz garlic
1 oz ginger
1 tablespoon mustard seeds
1 tablespoon peppercorns
1 tablespoon cumin seeds
½ tablespoon turmeric
1 tablespoon fenugreek
1 tablespoon plus 2 teaspoons chili powder
1 oz green (jalapeno or serrano) chilies
¾ bottle sesame or ground nut oil
10 *curry-pak* leaves
2 cups white vinegar
1 ½ cups sugar

*Preparation*
1. Cut the *brinjals* (eggplants) in fine pieces.
2. Salt and leave aside.
3. Grind the dry chilies with half the quantity of garlic and ginger, and the entire quantity of mustard seeds, peppercorns, cumin seeds, turmeric, fenugreek seeds and chili powder.
4. Cut the remaining ginger and garlic in small pieces and the green chilies into thick slices.
5. Heat the oil and add the *curry-pak* leaves, then the cut condiments. Cook for 2 minutes.
6. Add the ground spices, followed by sugar and vinegar and lastly the *brinjals.*
7. Cover and cook over low heat till the *brinjals* are a little softened; stirring all the time (this quantity requires an 11 inch pan).
8. When cool, bottle in sealed jars.

## Apple Chutney

*Ingredients*                                                                                    Preparation time: 20 minutes
                                                                                                                  Cooking time: 15 minutes

4 lb Jonathan apples
2 cups sugar
1 ⅓ cups white vinegar
2 teaspoons ginger (powder)
1 ½ teaspoons salt
6 oz seedless raisins
2 ½ teaspoons chili powder

*Preparation*
1. Peel and cut fine the apples.
2. Add the sugar and boil until a golden color.
3. Add the remaining ingredients and continue boiling (stirring all the time) until the required consistency.
4. Cool and put in sealed jars.

## Tomato Chutney

*Ingredients*                                                                                    Preparation time: 30 minutes
                                                                                                                  Cooking time: 15 minutes

1 cup white vinegar
6 dry (Goa) red or Kashmiri chilies
14 cloves garlic
1 inch piece ginger
Salt to taste
2 lb tomatoes, peeled and cut into small pieces
2 oz dried plums
1 cup sugar

*Preparation*
1. Grind in vinegar the chilies, garlic and ginger.
2. Add salt.
3. Combine the tomatoes, plums, sugar, in a saucepan with the ground spices, and boil until thick.
4. Cool and put in sealed jars.

# Coriander Leaves (Cilantro) Chutney

*Ingredients*  Preparation time: 15 minutes
Cooking time: 5minutes

1 bunch fresh coriander leaves (cilantro)
½ grated coconut (see "Useful Tips" section)
3 green (jalapeno or serrano) chilies, cut into strips
Pinch of cumin seeds
3 cloves of garlic, chopped
Pinch of ginger
1 onion roasted whole
Small ball of tamarind to yield about 2- 3 tablespoons of tamarind juice (see "Useful Tips" section)
Pinch of turmeric
Salt to taste
Sugar to taste

*Preparation*
1. Break off the coriander leaves from the stem.
2. Mix all the ingredients.
3. Put in blender and grind fine.
4. Add salt and sugar to taste.
5. Cool. Put in sealed jars and refrigerate.


# Carrot Pickle

*Ingredients*  Preparation time: 20 minutes
plus 3 days
Cooking time: 20 minutes

3 lb carrots (cut into thin strips)
1 tablespoon salt
3 lb sugar

Grind into a paste
    1-½ oz chili powder
    1-½ oz ginger
    1 ½ oz garlic

¾ bottle white vinegar (1 cup)
1 teaspoon cumin seeds (whole)

*Preparation*
1. Sun dry carrot strips with 1 tablespoon salt for 2 to 3 days.
2. Boil the carrots and sugar together over a slow fire.

3. When the carrots become transparent, add ground *masala* and vinegar and one teaspoon cumin seeds.
4. Bring to a boil two or three times.
5. Put in sealed jars and allow to cure for 2 weeks.

## G. Desserts, Sweets and Cookies

*Bebinca* – pictured on page 115

*Bôlo Podre* (Rotten Cake)

*Dedos de Dama* (Lady's Fingers) – pictured on page 115

*Alétria* – pictured on page 116

Coconut Cookies

Semolina and Coconut Cookies

Sweet Potato Dessert

*Dôce de Grão* (*Gram Dal* Sweet)

*Neureos*

*Dodol*

*Pinaca*

*Kulkuls*

*Cocada*

Chocolate Toffee

Lemon Tartlets

*Têias de Aranha* (Spider's Webs)

*Bôlo Sans Rival*

Orange and White *Blancmange* Dessert – pictured on page 116

*Omelata de Baunilha* (Vanilla Omelet)

*Pudim* Flan

Pineapple Whip

Banana Fritters (Banana Pancakes)

*Pasteis de Banana* (Banana Patties)

Coconut Pancakes

*Sooji* (Semolina) *Halva*

Carrot *Halva*

*Mangada* (Mango Jam)

*Jeleia de Goivas (*Guava Jelly)

## G. Desserts, Sweets and Cookies

The best known and loved Goan dessert is *bebinca*. It is wickedly rich and delicious, and it should be indulged in sparingly by those watching their cholesterol. If, however, one misses eating a piece of *bebinca*, one is depriving oneself of one of the essential components of Goan cuisine. No festive occasion is complete without *bebinca*.

Some of these sweets were always available at our home at Christmas: *kulkul*s, *gram dal* sweet, *dedos de dama*, coconut cookies, *neureos* and *alétria*, in addition, of course, to *bebinca*.

*Mangada* is a mango jam served at breakfast.

### *Bebinca* – pictured on page 115

*Ingredients*

Preparation time: 2 hours
Cooking time: 8 hours

8 cups sugar (diluted in 1 ½ cups water to make a syrup)
20 egg yolks lightly beaten
2 cups all-purpose flour
Milk of 2 coconuts (equal to 2 ⅔ cups of coconut milk) (see "Useful Tips" section)
½ lb butter
1 pinch salt
2 teaspoons vanilla essence

*Preparation*
1. Add the syrup to the beaten egg yolks a little at a time.
2. Then add, alternately, the flour and coconut milk, stirring to ensure that there are no lumps.
3. Stir in the salt and the vanilla.
4. Set the mixture aside for 30 minutes.
5. Preheat the oven to 350°F.
6. Place a tall cake mold with 3 oz of butter in the oven.
7. When the butter is melted, pour in 1 cup of the mixture and warm for 15 minutes.
8. Then change the oven to broil for 3 minutes to brown the top of the layer.
9. Now put a pan with hot water under the cake mold. Turn the oven temperature down to 250°F. Spread one tablespoon of butter evenly and add 1 cup of the mixture.
10. Repeat steps (8) and (9) above until the mixture is completely exhausted.
11. Remove the *bebinca* from the oven and let it cool.
12. Turn it over and unmold it. Garnish it with almond slivers, and decorate all around the rim with cut white paper.
13. Cut into fairly fine slices and serve.

## *Bôlo Podre*
(Rotten Cake)

*Ingredients*

Preparation time: 45 minutes
Cooking time: 60 minutes

1 lb sugar
½ cup water
1 coconut, grated fine (see "Useful Tips" section)
4 oz butter
3 tablespoons flour
10 egg yolks
2 egg whites
1 teaspoon vanilla essence
2 tablespoons sliced almonds
Butter for greasing pan
2 tablespoons sugar for sprinkling

*Preparation*
1. Mix the sugar with water and heat to make a thick syrup.
2. Add to the syrup the grated coconut and mix in well.
3. Remove from the stove, set aside for a few minutes. While still warm, mix in the butter and flour.
4. When cool, add in the egg yolks and lightly beaten egg whites, and the vanilla essence and sliced almonds. Mix well.
5. Grease a cake pan and sprinkle a bit of flour. Pour in the batter and ensure that it is evenly distributed.
6. Bake in an oven preheated to 350ºF until done.
7. Sprinkle 2 tablespoons sugar, slice, and serve.

## *Dedos de Dama* – pictured on page 115
(Lady's Fingers)

*Ingredients*

Preparation time: 2 days
Cooking time: 2 hours

4 ½ cups of grated coconut (see "Useful Tips" section)
½ cup ground almonds
2 cups sugar (diluted with 1 cup of water to make a syrup)
2 egg yolks
1 ½ teaspoons almond essence
4 cups sugar for coating
2 cups water

*Preparation*
1. Mix the coconut and almonds in the syrup and boil until sticky.
2. Cool the mixture; add the egg yolks and mix well.
3. Return the mixture to heat to cook the eggs. Add the almond essence.
4. When cool to the touch, shape the mixture into small (lady's) fingers.
5. Set aside for a day or so until completely dry before coating.
6. Caramelize at low heat 4 cups of sugar with 2 cups of water until light brown.
7. Dip the lady's fingers in the syrup to coat them lightly.
8. Set aside to cool. Serve. Each lady's finger can be pierced through with a serving pick, if so desired, or these can be put individually in tissue paper pastry cases.

## *Alétria* – *pictured on page 116*

*Ingredients*

Preparation time: 30 minutes
Cooking time: 25 minutes

2 ½ cups sugar (made into a syrup with 1½ cups of water)
8 -12 eggs with the yolks separated from the whites. Beat egg yolks and whites separately.
1 tablespoon butter
4 cups grated coconut (see "Useful Tips" section)
½ cup bread crumbs
1 pinch of salt
½ teaspoon vanilla
½ cup sliced almonds or cashew nuts
½ cup raisins

*Preparation*
1. Warm the syrup over low heat. Add the butter and melt it.
2. Using a cornet or pierced eggshell, gently pour the egg yolks into the syrup so as to form strings. Lightly cook the yolk strings and set them aside.
3. Put the grated coconut, bread crumbs, salt and vanilla into the syrup and cook until the syrup is completely absorbed. Add the beaten egg whites.
4. Put the cooked coconut mixture onto a serving dish. Decorate it by covering the coconut mixture entirely with the egg strings; sprinkle almonds and raisins on top of the egg strips.
5. Can be served either warm or cool.

# Coconut Cookies

Many coconut and potato sweet dishes were eaten at tea-time and were known by the Portuguese word "*merenda*". Some of these sweets also used *jaggery* (unrefined coconut sugar), instead of sugar.

*Ingredients*

Preparation time: 20 minutes
Cooking time: 40 minutes

12 egg whites (left over from preparing *Alétria*), well beaten
2 cups finely grated coconut (see "Useful Tips" section)
2 cups sugar, made into a syrup with 1 cup of water
½ cup flour
2 tablespoons butter
1 teaspoon almond essence
1 teaspoon vanilla essence

*Preparation*
1. Mix all the ingredients well to form a batter.
2. Butter a shallow cooking pan. Pour the batter into the pan and even it out.
3. Pre-heat the oven to 350ºF. Place the pan in the oven and cook until well brown.
4. Using cookie cutters, cut the cooked cake. Serve.

# Semolina and Coconut Cookies

*Ingredients*

Preparation time: 2 ½ hours
Cooking time: 1 hour

2 whole eggs
½ lb sugar
8 egg whites
½ lb semolina flour
1 grated coconut (see "Useful Tips" section)
½ teaspoon vanilla essence

*Preparation*
1. Beat the whole eggs with the sugar.
2. Stiffly beat the egg whites. Add these to the beaten whole eggs gradually, while continuing to beat the mixture.
3. Add the semolina, the grated coconut, and the vanilla essence. Mix in well. Set aside for about 2 hours.
4. In your hand, form small balls of the mixture. Place them on a buttered cookie dish.
5. Cook in an oven pre-heated to 300ºF for about one hour (until browned).
6. Cool and serve.

# Sweet Potato Dessert

*Ingredients*

Preparation time: 45 minutes
Cooking time: 20 minutes

4 medium size sweet potatoes, peeled and sliced into rounds
2 tablespoons of vegetable oil
1 grated coconut (see "Useful Tips" section)
1 cup sugar, made into a syrup with 1-1/2 cups of hot water
1 teaspoon vanilla essence

*Preparation*

1. Lightly fry the sweet potato slices in hot oil. Set aside on paper towels to absorb oil.
2. Cook the grated coconut in the hot syrup.
3. When the syrup is almost absorbed, add the potatoes and vanilla essence and mix gently (so as not to bruise the potatoes).
4. Serve hot.

# *Dôce de Grão*
## *(Gram Dal* Sweet*)*

*Ingredients*

Preparation time: 20 minutes
Cooking time: 15 minutes

½ lb sugar made into a syrup with 2 cups of hot water
1 grated coconut (see "Useful Tips" section)
¼ lb gram flour
6 crushed cardamom cloves
2 tablespoons vegetable oil
Butter for greasing cookie sheet

*Preparation*

1. Heat the syrup and add the coconut and gram flour.
2. While continuing to stir, add the cardamom and vegetable oil.
3. Take the mixture off the heat when it is of such a consistency that it does not stick to the sides of the cooking pot.
4. Pour onto a greased cookie sheet. Let cool.
5. Cut into desired shapes with a cookie cutter.
6. Sprinkle lightly with flour.
7. Store in a sealed container

## *Neureos*

*Ingredients* (24 neureos)

Preparation time: 45 minutes
Cooking time: 90 minutes

*For the pastry*
1 lb wheat flour
2 tablespoons vegetable oil
¼ teaspoon salt
Water for kneading dough

*For the filling*
½ lb sugar
½ cup water
1 coconut grated fine (see "Useful Tips" section)
2 tablespoons vegetable oil
¼ lb cashew nuts cut fine
6 cardamoms ground
¼ lb raisins

*Preparation*

1. To prepare the pastry: knead the flour, vegetable oil, salt with some water to form soft dough.
2. Divide the dough into 24 equal parts, and roll out a thin pastry in each case.
3. For the filling: Make a syrup of the sugar and water. Add the coconut, oil and nuts. Mix well and cook until not too dry. Add the cardamom and raisins and cook until the mixture is fairly dry.
4. When cool, add equal quantities of the filling to each pastry. Fold over the corners to form a half moon shape. Seal the edges with the tines of a fork.
5. Deep-fry the *neureos* in oil until golden.
6. Drain and cool on paper towels.
7. Cool and serve.


## *Dodol*

This recipe and the next one, *Pinaca*, are included here, for its regional interest, as the dessert is based on the coconut. It is rather difficult to duplicate in the US as the palm *jaggery*, which is a required ingredient, is seldom found in local stores.

*Ingredients*

Preparation time: 45 minutes
Cooking time: 30 minutes

2 coconuts grated (see "Useful Tips" section)
Water for coconut milk extraction
⅓ lb rice flour
1 lb coconut *jaggery* (unrefined coconut sugar)
¼ cashew nuts chopped

*Preparation*
1. Extract the milk from the coconut twice – the first is thicker than the second.
2. Mix the thinner coconut milk in a pot, add the rice flour, and at low heat, stir the mixture constantly, until it thickens.
3. Add the *jaggery* and mix well.
4. Then add the thick coconut milk. Stir for about 5 minutes and add the cashew nuts.
5. Cook while stirring, until the mixture is thick and does not cling to the edges of the pot.
6. Pour it into a serving dish to cool.
7. Cut in pieces and serve.

## **Pinaca**

*Ingredients*

½ lb uncooked rice
The white meat of a coconut, ground very fine (see "Useful Tips" section)
1 lb of palm *jaggery*
1 tablespoon brown sugar
Flour for coating the tart pans

*Preparation*
1. Toast the rice in a medium-hot skillet until the rice is brown. Do not let it burn. Grind it into flour.
2. In a heavy saucepan melt the *jaggery*, and when it has the consistency of thick molasses, add the sugar and stir until it is dissolved.
3. Add the ground coconut and the ground rice and blend well.
4. Lightly grease medium size individual tart pans and dust with a light coating of flour.
5. Pack the mixture into the tart pans and unmold when the mixture is relatively dry.

## ***Kulkuls***

This is a typical addition to the sweets offered at Christmas time. Traditionally, the whole family, especially the children, would participate in the preparation of the *Kulkuls*.

*Ingredients*                                   Preparation time: 45 minutes
                                                Cooking time: 20 minutes

¾ lb wheat flour
¼ lb semolina flour
1 tablespoon butter
4 egg yolks
Pinch of salt
½ cup thick coconut milk (see "Useful Tips" section)
Oil for frying the *kulkuls*
1 cup sugar
1 cup water

*Preparation*
1. Knead together well the wheat and semolina flour, butter, egg yolks, salt, and coconut milk to form a spongy dough.
2. Take a small pinch of dough and roll it on the tines of a fork or a fine comb to form a miniature croissant or conch shell (called a *kulkul*).
3. Use all the dough to form *kulkuls*.
4. Lightly deep-fry the *kulkuls* in hot oil.
5. Remove and dry on paper towels.
6. Prepare a syrup with the sugar and water. Dip the *kulkuls* in the syrup. While coating the *kulkuls* in syrup, add water as needed to prevent the syrup from crystallizing. Cool on a plate.
7. Store in an airtight container lined with paper.


## *Cocada*

*Ingredients*

Preparation time: 40 minutes
Cooking time: 25 minutes

½ lb sugar
1 cup water
1 finely grated coconut (see "Useful Tips" section)
⅓ lb semolina flour
1 teaspoon powdered cardamom

*Preparation*
1. In a pot, make a syrup of the water and sugar.
2. Pour in the grated coconut, the semolina flour and stir well.
3. Add the cardamom and stir until the mixture is thick enough not to cling to the sides of the pot.
4. Pour onto a greased cookie sheet. Cut in diamond shapes.
5. Cool and serve.


## **Chocolate Toffee**

This was a "must" at Christmas time. In fact, my mother would make one or two batches ahead of Christmas Day and then "hide" them in an airtight can in what she thought was a secret place. Unfortunately for her, the children were adept at discovering the can and consuming several, if not all, before the festive day.

*Ingredients*

Preparation time: 10 minutes
Cooking time: 30 minutes

½ powdered unsweetened cocoa
1 cup milk
2 cans (14 ½ oz each) sweetened condensed milk

2 cups sugar
2 teaspoons vanilla essence
2 tablespoons butter
Butter/margarine for greasing one cookie sheet
Walnut halves for decoration

*Preparation*
1. Thoroughly dissolve the cocoa in ½ cup of milk.
2. In a heavy saucepan, combine the condensed milk, the cocoa mixture and sugar.
3. Cook over a slow fire, stirring constantly, to the soft ball stage (238°F on the candy thermometer).
4. Stir in the vanilla and the butter.
5. Quickly pour on to the cookie sheet.
6. Score into small squares (about 2 inches across and ¼ inch thick). Smooth the top with a greased knife. Place a walnut half on each square.
7. When cool, separate the squares and store in an airtight tin.

## Lemon Tartlets

This is a variation of the tartlets to be found in the section on "Appetizers". Instead of savory, they are sweet and were used to serve drop-in visitors at tea-time or as part of a "high" tea. The tart molds are of the small size.

*Ingredients*                                      Preparation time: 30 minutes
                                                   Cooking time: 25 minutes

*For the crust:*
2 cups sifted all-purpose flour
1 teaspoon salt
½ teaspoon lemon peel (zest)
⅔ cup shortening
4 - 6 tablespoons chilled water
1 tablespoon lemon juice

*Preparation*
1. Sift the flour with the salt.
2. Stir in the lemon peel (zest).
3. Cut the shortening with a pastry blender or a fork, to the size of small peas.
4. Mix together the water with lemon juice.
5. Sprinkle 1 tablespoon of the liquid over a portion of the dry ingredients, mix lightly and push to the side of the bowl. Repeat this process 4-6 times, until the flour mixture is moistened.
6. Divide the dough into 2 portions. Form each portion into a ball. Flatten pastry balls, one at a time, onto a lightly floured surface. Roll from the center to the edge, in a circle, to a thickness of ⅛th of an inch.
7. Lightly grease the molds. Cut dough into shapes to line the molds with the pastry.
8. Bake in a 300°F oven.

*The Filling:*
4 eggs
½ cup sugar
1 ½ teaspoons lemon peel (zest)
6 tablespoons lemon juice
6 tablespoons chilled butter

*Preparation*
1. Whisk eggs, sugar, lemon peel (zest) and juice over very low heat, stirring constantly until the mixture is the consistency of thick hollandaise sauce (it should coat the back of a spoon and leave a definite track if you draw the back of the spoon across the top.) Do not let it get too stiff.
2. Add the chilled butter, cut into small pieces. Stir until the butter dissolves completely.
3. Pour into a chilled jar. May be refrigerated for up to 6 or 8 weeks. Stir before using. *Note:* the ratio of sugar to juice may have to be adjusted depending on the tartness of the lemon.
4. At serving time, fill the tartlets with the lemon curd filling and serve.

### *Têias de Aranha*
(Spider's Webs)

The key to this recipe is to get hold of a young tender coconut. This sweet was often made at Christmas-time or on religious holidays.

*Ingredients*                                           Preparation time: 60 minutes
                                                        Cooking time: 45 minutes

1 tender coconut
½ lb sugar
8 tablespoons of water
2 sheets of white tissue paper are required.

*Preparation*
1. Cut the tissue paper into squares or circles about 4 inches across. Spread the paper-shapes across a large counter.
2. Follow the directions in the "Useful Tips" section to get the white meat of the coconut. Remove the water and set aside.
3. Cut the white meat into strips about ¼ inch wide and 2 inches long and soak these in water while the syrup is being prepared.
4. In a medium-sized saucepan, on a slow fire, cook the sugar and water to make a syrup and add the drained coconut strips.
5. When the mixture thickens and begins to leave the sides of the pan, remove 2 or 3 strips at a time with a fork and a spoon and place on the tissue paper circles or squares and make a small pyramid shape. This must be done as quickly as possible as the syrup will harden in the pan. Sprinkle water into the syrup, as needed, to prevent crystallization.

### *Bôlo Sans Rival*

*Ingredients*

Preparation time: 20 minutes
Cooking time: 1 to 1 ½ hours

9 egg whites
12 oz sugar (1 ⅓ cups)
10 oz almonds (2 cups) powdered
2 tablespoons flour
Whipped cream
A few drops of vanilla essence
Toasted slivered almonds to garnish

*Preparation*
1. Beat the egg whites until stiff but not dry.
2. Mix half the sugar with the powdered almonds.
3. Lightly fold in the egg whites into the above alternately with the remaining half of sugar.
4. Add the 2 tablespoons of flour and blend.
5. Grease and flour two 10 x 5 inches pans or four smaller ones and bake at 300°F for approximately 1 to 1 ½ hours.
6. Sandwich the layers and cover the top and sides with whipped cream, beaten with a little vanilla and sugar to taste.
7. Garnish with toasted almonds.

### **Orange and White *Blancmange* Dessert** – *pictured on page 116*

*Ingredients* (6 servings)

Preparation time: 45 minutes
Cooking time: 10 minutes

6 (plus 2 to be kept in reserve) medium size tangerines (select fairly thick skinned ones)
6 tablespoons sugar (if the tangerines are sour, more sugar has to be added)
2 tablespoons powdered gelatin
1 ½ cups whole milk
Water to dissolve the gelatin

*Preparation*
1. With a sharp paring knife, cut a small round hole not more than ¾ inch in diameter from the top, stalk end of the tangerine, that is opposite the base. This is to enable the tangerines to stand on their own.
2. With the stem of a teaspoon, gently scoop out the fibers and remove the pulp of the tangerine, ensuring that the peel is not damaged. (Two extra tangerines are kept in reserve in case the peel/skin of any is damaged). Save the pulp.
3. When the pulp has been removed, carefully rinse the inside of the tangerines in water. Pour out the water, ensuring that there is no residue of fiber and pulp in the cases.
4. Pour fresh water into the cases and measure the amount of liquid necessary to fill the empty tangerine cases. Pour out the water. Turn the cases upside down to drain them

thoroughly and allow them to dry for ½ hour. The amount of tangerine juice needed is half the amount of liquid measured for the full tangerine cases.

5. Extract the juice of the tangerine pulp. This should approximately be about 1 ½ cups of juice. If it is less than half the liquid measured in the empty cases, then extract more tangerine juice from the tangerines kept in reserve, to make up the quantity of tangerine liquid needed.
6. Soak 1 tablespoon of gelatin in a little cold water for at least ½ hour.
7. On a low flame, heat the tangerine juice (do not allow it to come to a boil). When warm, add 3 tablespoons of sugar (or more) to the required sweetness. Add the gelatin and stir till it dissolves thoroughly.
8. Gently pour the tangerine and gelatin liquid into the tangerine cases to the half-way mark.
9. Place the cases on a plate and refrigerate overnight.
10. Soak ½ tablespoon of gelatin in cold water for about ½ hour.
11. Warm the milk and add 3 tablespoons of sugar.
12. Strain the milk and add a tablespoon of dissolved and strained gelatin.
13. Allow to cool thoroughly.
14. Remove the tangerine cases from the refrigerator and gently fill the remainder of each case with the milk mixture.
15. Refrigerate until set.
16. To serve, cut the tangerine cases vertically so that the two halves will have segments of orange and white.
17. Serve cold.

### *Omeleta de Baunilha*
*(Vanilla Omelet)*

This desert was a Goan favorite. It was made when guests arrived unexpectedly for lunch or for any family get-together. There is an option of using a wine sauce or a plain milk custard. This is a sweet version of the omelets eaten at breakfast.

*Ingredients*

*For the omelet*
10 eggs (separated)
5 oz sugar
1 teaspoon vanilla essence
Butter for greasing the Swiss roll pan (about 10 inches by 6 inches)

*For the wine sauce*
4 egg yolks
4 tablespoons sugar
4 tablespoons port wine

*or for a milk custard*
2 egg yolks
2 – 3 tablespoons sugar

Preparation time: 20 minutes
Cooking time: 15–20 minutes
plus 15 minutes for the sauce

2 cups milk
1 teaspoon vanilla essence for flavoring

*Preparation of omelet*
1. In a bowl, beat the egg yolks well with the sugar.
2. In another bowl, beat the egg whites stiff and dry.
3. Add the vanilla essence to the beaten egg whites and mix well.
4. Add the egg yolks to the egg white mixture.
5. Grease the baking pan. Cover with a sheet of wax/parchment paper. Grease the paper. Pour the mixture into the pan.
6. Bake in a preheated 300°F oven for 15 to 20 minutes until golden.
7. Flip the pan over a sheet of wax paper sprinkled with confectioners' sugar.
8. Gently roll the omelet into a Swiss roll. Place it in an attractive rectangular glass dish.
9. When cool, slice the omelet into slices of 1 inch to 1 ½ inches thick and pour the wine sauce (or milk custard) over it. Serve.

*Preparation of wine sauce*
1. Beat the egg yolks well with the sugar.
2. Add the port wine.
3. Cook over a slow fire until the sauce is thick, stirring continually. If the heat is too high, the eggs will scramble.

*Preparation of the milk custard*
1. Beat the egg yolks well with the sugar.
2. Cook on a slow fire until the sauce thickens, stirring continually.
3. Cool and add the vanilla essence.

## *Pudim* Flan

This was a dessert staple, especially on Sundays. European in origin, variations were introduced according to a household's desires. My mother made a coffee or a chocolate flan. In some homes, orange flavored flans were eaten, as they are, very often in Mexico.

*Ingredients* (6 – 8 servings)　　　　　　　　　　　　Preparation time: 30 minutes
　　　　　　　　　　　　　　　　　　　　　　　　　　Cooking time: 25-30 minutes

2 cups rich milk (half and half)
3 eggs
½ cup sugar
½ teaspoon vanilla essence
A 4-cup copper mold

*Preparation*
1. Bring ⅓ cup sugar and water to a boil in a small saucepan with a heat-proof handle.
2. Swirl the pan until the sugar has dissolved, and keep on the fire, swirling the pan frequently until the sugar has turned a rich caramel brown (about 3 minutes).

3. Pour the caramel immediately into the mold, and turn in all directions until the caramel adheres to bottom and sides of the pan. When the caramel ceases to run, place the mold upside down onto a plate.
4. Heat the milk until it simmers.
5. Beat together the eggs and the sugar, until the mixture is frothy. Gradually, add the hot milk in a thin stream, beating continually.
6. Add the vanilla essence.
7. Pour the mixture into the mold.
8. In a preheated oven to 350°F, place a large pan with very hot water, and set the mold in it. Bake for about 30 minutes. When the custard is done, a small knife plunged into the center should come out clean.
9. Remove from the pan with the water. Allow it to set for about 15 – 20 minutes. Run a knife around the inner edge of the mold and unmold on to a serving dish. Refrigerate and serve when cold.

*Note:* to make a chocolate flan, add 2 tablespoons of unsweetened cocoa to the milk when hot. The coffee flan requires 2 tablespoons of a high quality instant coffee.


### Pineapple Whip

Pineapples often grew in backyards in Goa. The one disadvantage of the pineapple plant is that it provides a perfect hiding place for snakes – so children were always warned to avoid them. A pineapple ripened on its bush has a singular flavor. Since it is not available year-round, canned pineapple was often used in this dessert.

*Ingredients* (8 servings)     Preparation time/cooking time
     45 minutes plus refrigeration

1 large can (14 oz) pineapple chunks or slices, in their own juice
3 oz cornstarch
3 oz sugar
4 eggs, separated
2 oz butter
Maraschino cherries and chopped walnuts for decoration

*Preparation*
1. Drain the pineapple thoroughly. Measure the juice, and add water if necessary, so that you have 3 cups of liquid.
2. In a small bowl, combine the cornstarch with sufficient juice to make a paste.
3. In a saucepan, bring the rest of the juice to a boil, add the sugar and the cornstarch paste, and cook, stirring continually until thick.
4. Remove from the fire, add the butter and the lightly beaten egg-yolks. Return to a medium-heat stove and cook again for 3 minutes.
5. Cool. While the mixture is cooling, beat the egg-whites into stiff peaks, and then fold them into the mixture. Pour into an appropriate serving dish.
6. Refrigerate for several hours.

7. In the meantime, cut the pineapple chunks into small pieces, saving a few whole ones to decorate the dessert. Refrigerate.
8. When ready to serve, fold in the cut pineapple pieces (do not add any of the juice) and then decorate the top with the reserved pineapple chunks, the cherries and the walnuts.

### Banana Fritters
(Banana Pancakes)

*Ingredients* (12 servings)

Preparation time: 20 minutes
Cooking time: 30 minutes

6 ripe medium size bananas
1 whole egg well-beaten
2 tablespoons sugar
2 tablespoons milk
2 heaped tablespoons all-purpose flour
½ teaspoon baking powder
Pinch of salt
2 tablespoons oil for frying
Sugar for sprinkling fritters (pancakes)

*Preparation*
1. Peel the bananas, and with a fork mash them well.
2. Mix all the ingredients, except the oil and sprinkling sugar, and add to the banana mixture. Set aside for at least ½ hour.
3. Heat a non-stick frying pan or griddle. Add the oil and heat it.
4. Pour 1 – 1 ½ tablespoons batter into the hot oil and fry until the edges brown.
5. Flip over and fry on the other side. Drain and set aside.
6. Fry individual fritters (pancakes) until all the batter is over.
7. Sprinkle with sugar and serve warm.

### *Pasteis de Bananas*
(Banana Patties)

*Ingredients*

Preparation time: 1 ½ hours
(for dough and filling)
Cooking time: 30 minutes

*For the banana jam filling*
12 ripe medium size bananas or 6 cups of mashed banana pulp
3 cups sugar
2 tablespoons butter
Butter for greasing the pan

*For the pastry dough*
3 cups all-purpose flour
½ cup butter

2 egg yolks
½ teaspoon salt
⅔ to ¾ cup thick coconut (see "Useful Tips" section)
Flour for sprinkling cookie sheet

*Preparation*

*Banana jam filling*
1. Mix the mashed banana pulp with the sugar and cook stirring continually, on a medium hot flame.
2. When the mixture is almost thick, add the 2 tablespoons of butter. Allow to cook until it attains the consistency of jam.
3. Transfer to a greased pan, set aside and allow to cool for at least 10 hours.

*Pastry dough*
1. Mix the flour and the butter, until the mixture resembles bread crumbs.
2. Add the 2 egg yolks and the salt.
3. Add the thick coconut milk to bind the ingredients together to form a soft dough. If the weather is dry, cover the dough with a damp cloth and allow to rest for an hour.
4. Take a ⅓$^{rd}$ portion of the dough, and roll it out into a thin pastry in a rectangular shape.
5. Cut strips from this rectangle about 2 inches wide.
6. Place a small (about 1 heaped teaspoon) ball of jam at the end of the strip and fold it in a triangular shape. Cut off from the strip of pastry dough. Twist the ends of the (*pastel*) patty to seal the dough.
7. Repeat step 6 until all the jam and the dough are used up.
8. Place the *pastries* (patties) on a flour sprinkled cookie sheet.
9. Pre-heat the oven to 375°F and bake till golden brown, for about 15 – 20 minutes.

## Coconut Pancakes

*Ingredients* (about 12 pancakes)    Preparation time: 30 minutes
                                     Cooking time: 20 minutes

1 coconut, grated
10 tablespoons sugar
¼ cup raisins (optional)
1 ½ teaspoons vanilla essence
½ teaspoon salt
1½ cups all-purpose flour
1 teaspoon baking powder
1 cup milk
1 cup water
2 eggs
½ teaspoon vegetable oil

*Preparation*
1. Mix the grated coconut with the sugar and cook on a slow fire until the coconut is soft and translucent. Throw in the raisins and remove from the fire. Add the vanilla essence and mix thoroughly. Keep aside.
2. Sift the flour with the baking powder. Mix the salt in the flour. Pour the milk, water, and lightly-beaten eggs over the flour and mix well.
3. Rub some of the oil on the bottom of a small (7 inch diameter) cast iron skillet. Heat it over medium high heat until it barely smokes.
4. Spread ¼ to ⅓ cup of the flour mixture in the heated skillet, swirling the liquid so that it covers the bottom of the pan in a thin film. Cook until the edges are dry and it comes loose from the side of the pan.
5. Turn the pancake over and let the other side cook for 30 seconds. When the pancake is ready, lift it from the skillet and place it in a plate.
6. Repeat the procedure until the flour batter is finished.
7. Put the coconut filling over half the pancake, and cover with the other half of the pancake.
8. Serve warm.

## *Sooji* (Semolina) *Halva*

Halva is a Middle Eastern dessert. Here we see the Muslim influence in Goa cooking. Semolina (*rulão*) is used in Portuguese dishes. Almonds grow in the Middle East as well as in the south of Portugal.

*Ingredients*                                       Preparation time: 30 minutes
                                                    Cooking time: 15–20 minutes

8 tablespoons butter
1 cup *sooji* (semolina)
2 cups cold water
2 cups sugar
1 cup milk
1 teaspoon almond essence
¼ teaspoon salt
A few drops of red and green food coloring
Sliced almonds or cashew nuts for decoration

*Preparation*
1. In a skillet melt one tablespoon of butter and fry the semolina until it is very light golden color.
2. In a saucepan, combine the semolina with the milk and the cold water and bring to a boil, stirring continually.
3. Stir in the salt.
4. Then add alternately, a little at a time, the butter and the sugar, making sure that these ingredients are thoroughly incorporated into the mixture, each time.
5. When the mixture begins to leave the sides of the pan, add the almond essence and the food color, and empty it into a flat serving dish.

6. Cool. Cut into diamond shapes and decorate with sliced almonds or chopped cashew nuts.

## **Carrot** *Halva*

This is a soft *halva* which has to be eaten by spoonful and not sliced.

*Ingredients*                                         Preparation time: 45 minutes
                                                      Cooking time: 20–30 minutes

1 lb carrots, cooked and finely shredded
1 ½ lb sugar
½ cup water
4 oz grated coconut (see "Useful Tips" section)
½ lb butter
2 or 3 crushed cardamom for flavor

*Preparation*
1. Make a thick syrup (about 225°F on a candy thermometer).
2. Mix in the carrots, coconut and butter, stirring thoroughly.
3. Add the crushed cardamom, if desired.
4. Cool.

## *Mangada*
(Mango Jam)

*Ingredients*                                         Preparation time: 20 minutes
                                                      Cooking time: 50 minutes

12 cups of pulp of ripe mangoes
5 cups sugar

*Preparation*
1. Mix the mango pulp and the sugar in a pot at low heat.
2. Cook stirring continuously until the mixture has the consistency of a jam.
3. Cool. Store in jam jars.
4. Serve as a breakfast jam, or spread on plain cookies and serve at tea time.

## *Jeleia de Goivas*
(Guava Jelly)

*Ingredients*

12 medium size ripe guavas
Water to cook the guavas
¾ cup sugar for each cup of liquid
Juice of 2 fresh sour limes

*Preparation*
1. Cut the guavas into halves, discard the stem bits, but leave in the seeds.
2. Place the guavas in a deep pan, cut side down.
3. Pour enough water to cover the guavas. If the guavas tend to float, place an overturned plate on top of them to keep them down.
4. Cook the guavas on a medium high flame till the liquid is reduced to one-third.
5. Over another pan, place a large sieve covered with a cheese cloth. Overturn the cooked guavas on the sieve, and allow them to drip for a couple of hours.
6. Measure the drained liquid. There should be no pulp in this liquid.
7. Add ¾ cup sugar for each cup of liquid.
8. Place the pan with the liquid on a medium high flame and cook until a little before it reaches the jelly stage (about 212°F on a candy thermometer). Add the lime juice.
9. When the liquid reaches 212°F, take it off the fire and allow it to cool for 10 minutes.
10. When still hot, pour into clean glass jars (which are set in a pan of cold water to prevent the jars from cracking when the hot liquid is poured into them).
11. Allow the jelly to cool thoroughly and then seal the jars.
12. Serve on toast, bread or plain cookies at breakfast or tea-time.

**Bebinca**

*Dedos de Dama (Lady's Fingers) and assorted sweets*

*Alétria*

*Dinner Table*

## H. Goan Drinks

Ginger Wine
*Orchata* (Almond Drink)
*Brindão (Kokum)* Syrup
Sour Lemon Syrup
Rose Syrup

## H. Goan Drinks

The drinks included in this section are generally served before meals or when there are visitors during the day. Ginger wine, a drink for which Alda Ribeiro Colaço was well known, was served as an "aperitif" or when visitors were received during the day. Men generally drink scotch whiskey, gin, vodka, or *feni* (a local eau-de-vie made of cashews or palm.) *Orchata* is a drink of European origin which is also found in Portugal, Spain, and Italy. It is generally served to women and children. *Brindão* (a fruit which is not available in the West) is a tart sweet drink which along with the Sour Lemon Syrup and the Rose Syrup are served at various times of the day to visitors.

Accompanying meals, we prefer to serve a dry rosé (Portuguese "Mateus" or French Rosé d'Anjou) or a dry white wine. The wine should complement the pungency and spiciness of the dishes being served.

### Ginger Wine

*Ingredients*

Preparation time: 30 minutes
Cooking time: 30 minutes

15 cups boiling water
½ oz essence cinnamon (or whole cinnamon)
10 cups sugar
½ oz tartaric acid (available in chemical supply store)
½ oz essence ginger
Juice of 6 limes
½ cup granulated sugar to caramelize
2 ½ tablespoons water

*Preparation*
1. Boil water with cinnamon.
2. Add sugar and tartaric acid to boiling water.
3. Let cool.
4. Add essence of ginger and lime juice.
5. Add the caramel (see below).

*Caramel for coloring ginger wine*
1. In a small saucepan, combine the sugar and water and bring to a boil, slowly shaking and swirling the pan until the sugar has dissolved.
2. Boil, swirling the pan frequently until the sugar has turned a rich caramel brown – about 2 or 3 minutes.
3. Use as much as needed *immediately* to give the wine a lovely amber color. Note: if the caramel is not used immediately, it will harden. Store the remainder in a jar in the refrigerator.
4. Bottle and keep the ginger wine for 10 days before drinking.

## *Orchata*
(Almond Drink)

*Ingredients*                                   Preparation time: 25 minutes
                                                Cooking time: 10 minutes

¼ lb almond
½ cup water
¼ lb sugar
½ teaspoon almond essence

*Preparation*
1. Grind the almonds with water to a fine consistency, so as to make an emulsion.
2. Make a thick syrup of the sugar with a little water.
3. Add the almond emulsion and bring to a boil.
4. Remove from the heat and cool. Add almond essence.
5. Store in dry bottles.
6. Serve by adding water and ice.

## *Brindão* Syrup
(*Kokum* Syrup)

*Ingredients*                                   Preparation time: 60 minutes

Enough *brindão* (*kokum*) fruit to extract 3 cups of *brindão* juice
Water to boil the *brindão* fruit
3 cups sugar
3 cups water
5 teaspoons citric acid (available in chemical supply stores)
¾ teaspoon sodium benzoate

*Preparation*
1. Wash the fruit. Boil in a little water to soften the fruit.
2. Drain the water. Cut the fruit and remove the seeds.
3. Using a straining cloth, strain the pulp and capture the juice.
4. Grind the seeds and strain and keep the juice.
5. Mix both kinds of juice (fruit juice and seed juice of *brindão* (*kokum*)).
6. Heat the sugar, water and citric acid, stirring until the sugar has completely dissolved.
7. When lukewarm, mix in the juice.
8. Mix the sodium benzoate in a small amount of the mixture, and add back this preservative to the mixture and stir well.
9. Bottle. Use as a refreshing summer drink by diluting 3 oz of syrup to 5 - 6 oz of water.

## Sour Lemon Syrup

*Ingredients*

12 green lemons
4 cups of sugar
3 cups of water
2 tablespoons of tartaric acid (available in chemical supply stores)

*Preparation*
1. Extract the juice of the lemons (about 2 ¾ to 3 cups), and set aside.
2. Combine the sugar and the water in a saucepan and make a thick syrup.
3. Cool. Add the tartaric acid and pass through a strainer.
4. Add the lemon juice and bottle. Keep refrigerated.
5. Use as a concentrate, diluted with water and ice at serving time.

*Note:* If tartaric acid is not available, the juice should be consumed within 15 days. Otherwise it may be kept for up to 2 months.

## Rose Syrup

*Ingredients*

6 cups sugar
3 cups water
2 scant teaspoons of citric acid (available in chemical supply stores)
2 teaspoons of essence of rose (found in ethnic stores)
A few drops of red food coloring

*Preparation*
1. Boil together the sugar and the water to make a thick syrup.
2. Add the citric acid. Allow to cool, than add the rose essence and the food coloring.
3. Bottle. Keep refrigerated.
4. Use as a concentrate, diluted with water and ice at serving time.

# INDEX OF RECIPES

**Useful tips**

|   |   |   |
|---|---|---|
| a) | grated coconut | 20 |
| b) | coconut milk | 20 |
| c) | *mirem* or *masala* | 20 |
| d) | garlic-ginger paste | 21 |
| e) | tamarind juice | 22 |

**A. Soups and Appetizers**

<u>Soups</u>

| | | |
|---|---|---|
| 1. | Basic Chicken Stock | 24 |
| 2. | Basic Beef Stock | 25 |
| 3. | *Canja/Pez* (Rice Soup) | 26 |
| 4. | *Canja de Galinha* (Chicken and Rice Soup) | 26 |
| 5. | *Caldo Verde* (Green Soup) | 27 |
| 6. | Coriander Leaf (Cilantro) Soup | 27 |
| 7. | Coriander Leaf (Cilantro) and Green Pea Soup | 28 |
| 8. | Cucumber Soup I | 28 |
| 9. | Cucumber Soup II | 29 |
| 10. | Vegetable Soup | 29 |
| 11. | Asparagus Soup | 30 |
| 12. | *Dal* (Lentil) Soup | 30 |
| 13. | *Sopa de Camarão* (Prawn Soup) | 31 |
| 14. | Bacon Soup | 31 |

<u>Appetizers</u>

| | | |
|---|---|---|
| 15. | *Rissoes de Camarão* (Prawn Puffs) | 33 |
| 16. | *Fofos de Peixe* (Fish Rolls) | 34 |
| 17. | *Empadinhas* (Small Pork Pies) | 35 |
| 18. | *Fofos de Queijo* (Cheese Puffs) | 36 |
| 19. | Shrimp Toast | 36 |
| 20. | *Forminhas* (Tartlets) | 37 |
| 21. | Meat Patties | 37 |

**B. Fish and Seafood**

| | | |
|---|---|---|
| 1. | *Peixe Recheado* (Mackerels Stuffed with Spices) | 40 |
| 2. | *Ambot Tik* (Sour and Hot Fish) | 41 |
| 3. | Goa Fish Curry | 41 |
| 4. | Prawn Cutlets | 42 |
| 5. | *Peixe Vermelho* (Red Fish) | 43 |
| 6. | *Pará dePeixe* (Sour Fish) | 43 |
| 7. | *Thisrio* (Clams) | 44 |
| 8. | *Sunkattam Koddi* (Prawn Curry) | 45 |
| 9. | *Apa de Camarão* (Prawn Pie) | 45 |
| 10. | *Poios* (Small Prawn Patties) | 46 |
| 11. | *Empada de Ostras* (Oyster Pie) | 47 |
| 12. | *Bombil Fish* (Fried Fresh *Bombay Duck*) | 48 |
| 13. | *Sukhe Bombil* (Dried *Bombay Duck*) | 48 |
| 14. | Sauteed Prawns | 49 |

| | |
|---|---|
| 15. Squid | 49 |
| 16. Salmon Aspic | 50 |
| 17. Salmon Cutlets | 51 |

**C. Meats and Poultry**

| | |
|---|---|
| 1. *Xacuti* | 56 |
| 2. Chicken Curry | 57 |
| 3. *Sarapatel* | 57 |
| 4. *Cabidela* | 58 |
| 5. *Carne de Balchão* (Pork with Shrimp Paste) | 59 |
| 6. Veal Tongue with White Sauce | 60 |
| 7. Potato Chops | 60 |
| 8. Beef Cutlets | 61 |
| 9. Beef Croquettes | 62 |
| 10. Pork *Vindalho* | 63 |
| 11. *Chouriço* | 63 |
| 12. Beef Roll | 64 |
| 13. *Bife em Sangue* (Pan-Broiled Steak) | 65 |
| 14. *Empada de Carne de Porco* (Pork Pie) | 65 |
| 15. *Lingua Salgada* (Salted Beef Tongue) | 66 |

**D. Vegetables and Eggs**

| | |
|---|---|
| 1. *Dudhi* (Pumpkin) | 70 |
| 2. *Tantiam Koddi* (Egg Curry) | 70 |
| 3. Potato *Bhaji* | 71 |
| 4. Spinach I | 71 |
| 5. Spinach II | 72 |
| 6. *Vadde Bhaji* | 72 |
| 7. Baked Spinach Casserole | 73 |
| 8. Okra I | 74 |
| 9. Okra II | 74 |
| 10. Okra with Grated Coconut | 75 |
| 11. *Brinjal* (Eggplant) Casserole | 76 |
| 12. *Brinjal Botha* (Pureed Eggplant) | 77 |
| 13. Layered *Brinjal* (Eggplant) Casserole with Coconut Sauce | 77 |

**E. Rice and Breads**

| | |
|---|---|
| 1. *Basmati* Rice (Steamed Long-Grain Rice) | 80 |
| 2. *Arroz Refugado* | 80 |
| 3. *Congee (Pez)* | 81 |
| 4. *Arroz Arabe* | 81 |
| 5. *Sannas* (Goan *Idlis*) | 82 |
| 6. Green *Pulao* | 82 |
| 7. *Oddes (Puris)* | 83 |
| 8. *Açorda de Pão* | 83 |

**F. Chutneys and Pickles**

| | |
|---|---|
| 1. *Capsicum* (Bell Pepper) Pickle I | 86 |
| 2. *Capsicum* (Bell Pepper) Pickle II | 87 |
| 3. Lime Pickle | 87 |
| 4. *Tendlim* Pickle (Small Gherkins Pickles) | 88 |
| 5. Mango Chutney | 89 |

| | |
|---|---|
| 6. Mango *Miscut* (Spicy Mango Pickle) | 89 |
| 7. *Chepnim Ambli* (Tender Green Mangoes Cured in Salt) | 90 |
| 8. Prawn *Balchão* (Pickled Prawns) | 90 |
| 9. *Brinjal* (Eggplant) Pickle | 91 |
| 10. Apple Chutney | 92 |
| 11. Tomato Chutney | 92 |
| 12. Coriander Leaves (Cilantro) Chutney | 93 |
| 13. Carrot Pickle | 93 |

**G. Desserts, Sweets and Cookies**

| | |
|---|---|
| 1. *Bebinca* | 96 |
| 2. *Bôlo Podre* (Rotten Cake) | 97 |
| 3. *Dedos de Dama* (Lady's fingers) | 97 |
| 4. *Alétria* | 98 |
| 5. Coconut Cookies | 99 |
| 6. Semolina and Coconut Cookies | 99 |
| 7. Sweet Potato Dessert | 100 |
| 8. *Dôce de Grão* (*Gram Dal* Sweet) | 100 |
| 9. *Neureos* | 101 |
| 10. *Dodol* | 101 |
| 11. *Pinaca* | 102 |
| 12. *Kulkuls* | 102 |
| 13. *Cocada* | 103 |
| 14. Chocolate Toffee | 103 |
| 15. Lemon Tartlets | 104 |
| 16. *Têias de Aranha* (Spider's Webs) | 105 |
| 17. *Bôlo Sans Rival* | 106 |
| 18. Orange and White *Blancmange* Dessert | 106 |
| 19. *Omeleta de Baunilha* (Vanilla Omelet) | 107 |
| 20. *Pudim* Flan | 108 |
| 21. Pineapple Whip | 109 |
| 22. Banana Fritters (Banana Pancakes) | 110 |
| 23. *Pasteis de Banana* (Banana Patties) | 110 |
| 24. Coconut Pancakes | 111 |
| 25. *Sooji* (Semolina) *Halva* | 112 |
| 26. Carrot *Halva* | 113 |
| 27. *Mangada* (Mango Jam) | 113 |
| 28. *Jeleia de Goivas* (Guava Jelly) | 113 |

**H. Goan Drinks**

| | |
|---|---|
| 1. Ginger Wine | 118 |
| 2. *Orchata* (Almond Drink) | 119 |
| 3. *Brindão (Kokum)* Syrup | 119 |
| 4. Sour Lemon Syrup | 120 |
| 5. Rose Syrup | 120 |

# Menus

## *Sunday Lunch with Family Members*

Soup broth with vegetables or vermicelli
A meat dish: cutlets, veal tongue, *xacuti* of chicken
One vegetable
*Arroz refugado* accompanied with *papads*, *chouriços*,
pickles or chutney, fried prawns with onions
A cream dessert with fruit (pineapple, sweet limes or sliced melon with sugar

## *Sit down dinner*

A light soup
A fish dish with salad
A meat dish – chicken with potato puree or a vegetable
*Arroz refugado* or *basmati* rice with a chicken curry, served with
pomfret or fried prawns and other accompaniments
A dessert pudding
Coffee served in demitasse cups

## *Festive lunch (Feast Day, Christmas, Easter or a birthday)*

This generally includes a sizeable number of guests and was generally a buffet

3 kinds of appetizers
followed by a broth

The buffet table is laid out with
A fish or seafood (prawns, oysters, squid, crab, etc.)
Meat dish: veal tongue, and chicken
*sarapatel* with *sannas*
Salads and vegetables
*Arroz refugado* with accompaniments
3 or four kinds of desserts: *bebinca*, puddings, tarts, pies, etc.

## **Wedding Meal**

On arrival, each guest receives a plate with 5 kinds of hors d'oeuvres (*rissoes*, cheese puffs, stuffed pastry shells, croquettes, etc.)

A little later broth is served in soup cups.

The buffet generally has

- 2 or 3 kinds of fish dish (fish with mayonnaise, fried fish filets with sauce, fish *balchão*, etc.)

- prawns, either fried with a sauce, *apa de Camarão*, *vindaloo* of prawns
- seafood: mussels, crab in the shell
- meats: *xacuti*, *sarapatel* with *sannas*, roast pork
- various salads and vegetables
- *arroz refugado* with accompaniments

There is a separate dessert table with at least a dozen different sweets: *bebinca*, *bôlo sans rival*, *alétria*, puddings, *dedos de dama*, ice creams, chocolate mousse, etc.

Wines and alcohols accompany the meals.

# GLOSSARY

| | |
|---|---|
| Bacalhau | cod fish |
| Balcão | veranda |
| Balichão | dried shrimp paste |
| Bhaji | a vegetable curry without gravy |
| Bilimbim | vegetable similar to French cornichon (gherkins) |
| Bombay Duck (Bombil | local fish which has no equivalent in the Western Hemisphere |
| Brindão | Called *Kokum*. It is available in ethnic stores. |
| Brinjal | eggplant, aubergine |
| Camarão | shrimp, prawn |
| Congee (canja) | rice broth |
| Chepniche Amblim | pickled green mango |
| Chutney | savory or sweet pickled fruits or vegetable used to accompany meals |
| Dal | lentils |
| Feni | cashew or palm eau-de-vie |
| Galinha | chicken |
| Ghee | clarified butter |
| Idlis | South Indian rice cakes |
| Jaggery | unrefined coconut sugar |
| Konkani | local language of Goa |
| Masala | a blended combination of spices |
| Garam Masala | A blend of cumin, pepper, cloves & cardamom |
| Mesta | cook/chef |
| Mirem | blended combination of garlic, chilies, turmeric, cumin seeds, coriander seeds, tamarind, (sometime ginger) and vinegar. |
| Pez | Konkani for rice broth (congee in English and canja in Portuguese) |
| Puris (Oddes) | Rice flour puffs |
| Sura | palm toddy |
| Xitt Koddi | Curry with rice |